# On Sibyl's Shoulders

## *Seeking Soul in Library Leadership*

Donna Brockmeyer

The Scarecrow Press, Inc.
Lanham, Maryland • Toronto • Oxford
2005

# SCARECROW PRESS, INC.

Published in the United States of America
by Scarecrow Press, Inc.
A wholly owned subsidiary of
The Rowman & Littlefield Publishing Group, Inc.
4501 Forbes Boulevard, Suite 200, Lanham, Maryland 20706
www.scarecrowpress.com

PO Box 317
Oxford
OX2 9RU, UK

British Library Cataloguing in Publication Information Available

**Library of Congress Cataloging-in-Publication Data**
Brockmeyer, Donna, 1961–
  On Sibyl's shoulders : seeking soul in library leadership / Donna Brockmeyer.
    p. cm.
  Includes bibliographical references and index.
  ISBN 0-8108-5120-2 (pbk. : alk. paper)
  1. Library administration—Social aspects. 2. Library science—Social aspects.
3. Leadership. 4. Quality of work life. 5. Libraries—Sociological aspects. I.
Title.
  Z678.B8185 2005
  025.1—dc22

                                                    2005006307

⊖™ The paper used in this publication meets the minimum requirements of
American National Standard for Information Sciences—Permanence of
Paper for Printed Library Materials, ANSI/NISO Z39.48-1992.
Manufactured in the United States of America.

# Tribute

Late one evening while I was working on this book, my husband, Brad, appeared at the garden door. Reaching for my hand, he drew me out into the cool September air. He motioned skyward and showed me the most spectacular and gracious Northern Lights (Aurora Borealis) I had ever seen. We awakened our son, Zackary, so that he, too, might see the splendor of this sight.

As the vision danced and swept the sky, we thought it appeared as a winged eagle in flight. With my feet planted in the garden, I saw, with the aid and company of my family, a bird in flight whose wings touched the horizon.

I thank Brad and Zack for giving me my greatest gifts:

- For Roots—Zack's joy has taught me to love and his sense of humor has taught me to laugh, while Brad's support has sustained me through three degrees and this book
- And for Wings—with which to fly.

*I thank you*

# Contents

# Acknowledgments

**I thank:**

Mr. Ernie Ingles, who has been for me first and foremost, a dear friend, a teacher, an inspiration and a mentor. Through Northern Exposure to Leadership (NEL), he modeled how to cast a vision and catch its reality. I thank him for supporting me in my professional career and for urging us all to not go gentle into that good night—to rage against the dying of the light (Dylan Thomas, 1952). **From Northern Exposure to Leadership and Snowbird Leadership Institutes:** Pat Cavill, Trevor Hamans, and Karen Adams, for their friendship and leadership as well as all of the participants and mentors at NEL. Margaret Andrewes, Becky Schreiber, John Shannon and the late J. Dennis Day for their work at Snowbird. **The Leaders Profiled in This Book:** Mr. Ernie Ingles, Dr. Ken Haycock, Dr. Marianne Scott, Ms. Bridget Lamont, Mr. Stephen Abram, Ms. Jo Bryant, Dr. Scott Bennett, Mr. James Neal and Ms. Vivienne Monty. **From St. Thomas More College (STM):** Dr. George Smith, CSB, President of STM who has an inclusive vision of leadership and an expanded vision of libraries, and my Library Assistant, Mrs. Dorothy Abernethy, who supported my work practically and sustained my soul spiritually. **Doctoral Committee and Cohort:** From the University of British Columbia, I thank Dr. Shauna Butterwick and Dr. Tom Sork, my supervisors, as well as the doctoral cohort who encouraged me. **Extended Family:** I thank my parents, Ted and Clara Brockmeyer, and my siblings, Carol, Karen, Joyce, Murray, Arlene, Ted and James, who gave me courage, as well as Zackary's grandparents, Lois and Lawrence Klebaum, for caring for Zack while I wrote. **Lifelong Soulmates:** I thank my dear friends Carolyn Brooks, Grace Carney, Joanne Butler, Erika Ritchie, Colleen Krushelinski, Pilar Martinez and Delia Stephens; these are women who heard my soul singing even when it was silent, and with whom I blissfully tossed pearls of drunken wisdom into goblets of red wine. **Kindred Spirit:** Finally, I sincerely thank my dear friend Michael Burgess, the great Canadian tenor of Les Miserables and other works, who inspires me to create the life of my dreams and to dream big knowing that all things are possible.

*I am blessed to know each of you.*

# Chapter One

# The Soul in Library Leadership

*The library is a house of healing for the soul.*
—King Ramses I

Libraries have been characterized as houses of healing, hearts of academies, commons of communities, and places of wonder, magic, learning and growth. Clearly, with such lauding, those who work in them are all leaders. This book is about professional and organizational leadership, as well as the way in which leadership is nurtured within all levels and forms of librarianship. It assumes leadership from all, regardless of formal role or organizational position. In an information-based economy with increasing social expectations from both employers and clients, all are called to lead. This book, then, is about you and me, and also, about those who have stood out among us as visionaries, mentors, and role models. It offers a glimpse into those so known, so that we can appreciate more fully their gifts and their challenges, and in doing so, it illuminates for us the many similarities between all of us who work toward creating meaningful work and making a difference through our efforts. It calls us to recognize that there are as many different ways to lead as there are leaders and that we cannot be content to let others take on the task of leadership—we are all called to step up to the mark. There is no *them* upon whom to rely; there is only *us*.

With that perspective, all of us who work in libraries engage in various ways in the work of Sibyl. Greek antiquity suggests that Sibyl was a mighty and strong female prophet who had, and wrote about, divine knowledge of the coming and the life of the Messiah. David Potter tracks a number of variations of the myth of Sibyl to the first century B.C. work of scholar Terentius Varro. Varro lists ten Sibyls: Babylonian, Libyan, Delphic, Cimmerian, Samian, Phrygian, Tiburtine, Erythraean, Cumaean and Hellespontine, each with her own story. According to

Filippo Barbieri, as related by Frederick Hartt in *Michelangelo* (p. 120), the Libyan Sibyl, Libica, prophesied:

> Behold, the day shall come and shall illuminate the condensed shadows, and the lips of men shall be silent: and they shall see the King of the Living. A virgin, the mistress of the nations, shall hold him in her lap, and shall reign in mercy; and the womb of his mother shall be the image of all.

Sibyl wrote of these prophesies, and it is attributed to another Sibyl, the Cumaean Sibyl, who wrote her prophesies in nine books, which she tried to sell to Tarquin, the last of seven kings of Rome. Tarquin refused to pay the requested price. Consequently, Sibyl burned first three of her books and then three more, at which time Tarquin paid the full price requested for the nine, but received only the three which remained. The books were kept at the capitol in Rome and were consulted in various forms until the fourth century A.D. According to legend, Sibyl was much loved by Apollo, who granted her years of life consistent with the grains of sand held in her hand, but as she continued to refuse him, he doomed her to look her age. The depiction of the Sibyl on the cover of this book is that of the Libyan Sibyl, young and beautiful, while Michelangelo's Cumaean Sibyl on the Sistine Chapel is immensely old. Another of the Sibyls is the Erythraean Sibyl, whose writings describe the Last Judgement and the Passion of Christ. Sibyl, in various depictions at various ages and stages of life, is portrayed as a prophet and an "every woman" of courage and conviction who believed in the power of her vision and the power of the book. She models for librarians strength of character in making difficult choices, tenacity in meeting her objective to make a difference, and belief in the power of information and the book in shaping the future of our world. When it is said that leaders, any of us, stand on the shoulders of giants when we do our work, we certainly stand on hers.

The expansive and inclusive conception of leadership in this book is reflected in a discussion about aspects of ancient, contemporary, critical, feminist and alternative leadership. Theory is enriched by profiles and individual narrative from nine

North American library leaders. These library directors, national librarians and library association presidents (current or past) consider aspects of leadership including but not limited to: vision, passion, advocacy, courage, initiative, ethics, stewardship, instincts, and balance between work and the rest of life. This book is also premised upon my doctoral studies at the University of British Columbia, Canada, concerning library leadership institutes and is focused primarily on the Northern Exposure to Leadership Institute commonly referred to as NEL in Canada as well as the Snowbird Leadership Institute in the United States. Ultimately, this research and writing is intended to both describe and enrich our understanding of ways to create meaning and deep satisfaction in the workplace for all, regardless of leadership role or organizational position.

This broad explication of library leadership is rendered in this book through the metaphor of the soul. As such, it is a book about you and me in our work and in our lives and what occurs within and between each of us and those we serve. In this, it allows for a wonderfully vast way of being, which celebrates all aspects of our humanity, for:

> Soul . . . makes a place for depth as well as height, for failure as well as triumph, for weakness as well as strength, for infirmity as well as health, for poverty as well as riches, for wisdom as well as knowledge, for woundedness as well as healing, for flaws as well as perfection, for depression as well as joy, for the loser as well as the winner, for the beaten as well as the triumphant, for the outcast as well as the accepted, for the downtrodden as well as the privileged, for tears as well as laughter, for roots as well as wings, and even for death as well as life. Soul enters when our spirits have been crushed and our egos have fallen apart. She moves gently and quietly amid the ruins of a destroyed life and begins to build again. She stays with us when everyone else has left and holds us through the night until the dawn breaks again. Through the night, she sings us songs we have never heard yet somehow know by heart. She tells us stories of courage, not the courage of dashing heroes and heroines but a deeper courage that only grows in the valleys of defeat and despair. In the cracks of our shattered lives, she plants the painful seeds of hope. All this is the work of the soul. (Elkins, 1995, p. 86)

This conceptualization of library leadership is rendered through the metaphor of soul in order to add a dimension to our work and to our lives that many historians believe has been lost, is long overdue and is much needed as many people today long for meaning.

## Historical Aspects of Conceptions of Soul

William Barrett, in *Death of the Soul* (1986), explores the evolution of the human understanding of mind, consciousness and faith in the divine and the decline of the soul by exploring evolution from the beginnings of the New Science and mechanization to the present. Mechanization experiments with and explores matter that has been thoroughly schematized, abstracted and mathematicized but does not explore it in its fullest multidimensional aspects, wherein the whole is more than the sum of its parts. Scientific materialism has become the dominant mentality of the West and rules not so much as an explicit and articulate philosophy, but more potently as an unspoken attitude, habit and prejudice of the mind. Barrett claims that technology exists within scientific materialism, wherein the very being of humanity is reduced to mechanization and humans are presented as extensions of machines, or as cogs within them. This is what Charlie Chaplin attempted to portray in the film *Modern Times* (1936). In this film, Chaplin depicts machines, in the construction of material objects, as having greater importance than those humans who operate the equipment. In this view of the world, humans and their souls become secondary to mechanization.

While Chaplin's film is set in the first half of the 1900s, it can be argued that humans are still as entrapped and secondary to production (mechanized or intellectual) at the close of the twentieth century. Employing Marshall McLuhan, Robert Sardello (1992) offers an explication of the ways in which technology has left us devoid of soul and suggests that it renders us divorced from deeper elements of ourselves and the world around us. He argues that with mechanical technology, parts of the body are extended into the world. For example, the wheel is both an extension and an acceleration of walking, which leaves us unable to cope with the increased pace because it disturbs the senses. With electronic technology, the brain is exteriorized into the world resulting in disorientation and a false sense of feeling personally connected with and able to view and understand the world. Yet, this is an illusion. With television, for example, while viewers believe they see a picture, they merely see electronic dots on a screen. If television damages the soul, he argues, it is not because of content, but because of the medium, which viewers forget is a momentary, synthetic world of which they are not an active part. They not only then live within an illusion, they have an inflated view of the power of technology. He alerts us to the inherent dangers in this by casting his explication in the light of the movie *Blade Runner*, in which technology is highly advanced. The world depicted in *Blade Runner*, however, was a horrible disaster: electronic gates blocked garbage strewn streets where seedy characters lurked. He also reminds us of the change of heart of scientists such as Pascal, who invented the calculator which is a predecessor to the computer. Pascal, after a brilliant scientific career, experienced the power of soul and a being greater than himself. Upon this encounter, he relinquished his scientific work (Sardello, 1992). Sardello suggests that the manic urge to create a technological world arises when the soul can no longer be felt as a creative force in the world, which is not to say that technology is inherently evil, just that it sometimes displaces more soulful considerations. This mania can only be balanced by strengthening the forces of soul, and nurturing a conjoining of all souls to create a world soul which can similarly be done, I believe, within the microcosm of a profession such as librarianship.

Paradoxically, while the human mind has created technologies, scientific methodologies and science itself, it has not left us the tools to understand fully the human mind, or the more subtle dimensions of our existence. Barrett notes:

In the three and a half centuries since modern science entered the world, we have added immeasurably to our knowledge of physical nature, in scope, depth, and subtlety. But our understanding of human consciousness in this time has become fragmentary and bizarre. (Barrett, 1986, p. xvi)

Yet, Barrett suggests, for Christians in the seventeenth century, there was a special exemption for the soul. It was not a natural phenomenon; it stood outside of nature. But the effect of this placement was to leave the soul "perched precariously on the edge of matter." While soul is not detectable to our physical senses it can be likened to an aroma that permeates all things. Given that soul was not detectable, nor quantifiable, there is little wonder that it has been displaced in a world that measures and values that which has material elements.

Barrett places the dislocation of soul within a broader context of human understanding of our place, or displace, within the universe. Over time, we became aware of the vastness of the cosmos, and that we were neither at the center nor the edge of it, but merely a small planet nowhere in particular in a teeming universe. A growing sense of cosmic alienation, a driving force of scientific materialism and a growing ideology of scientism have left us floundering about without a foundation upon which to build or even retain a sense of soul. The nineteenth century had begun to recognize this loss, and religion, myth, magic and philosophy have all begun to grapple with it, suggests Barrett. I would add, so too have counselors, teachers, writers, poets, and artists—as well as taxi drivers, doctors, homemakers, lawyers and librarians. In short, all of us have.

Caitlin Matthews, in *Singing the Soul Back Home* (1995), suggests that in addition to common needs, such as health, work, and relationships, we also have needs resulting from urban Western life. This includes the need to address soul-loss, which is manifest in feelings of incompleteness and meaninglessness, alienation, addiction, and lack of self-esteem and vision on a personal as well as a social level: we suffer from poverty, oppression, war, terrorism, racism, exclusion, ignorance, sexism, materialism, and consumerism. Even our ecosystem suffers.

"Western society allows us to be aware in our body and in our mind; it sometimes permits us to be aware in our psyche, but it gives no importance to soul, parts of which have become homeless" (Matthews, 1995, p. 25). While modern medicine and psychiatry deal with what they see as mental illness, and the criminal justice system and the welfare state try to cope with social ills, the more subtle aspects of distress and imbalance are ignored or marginalized. Matthews (1995) ponders:

> What of those who believe there is no subtle reality? These are a strange tribe, the first of their kind in the history of world anthropology. We live in extraordinary times when people disbelieve in spiritual worlds and beings. This total disregard for subtle reality makes it very hard for the mystics and visionaries who perceive it to live in our society. I am not speaking of people of extraordinary gifts, but of everyone who experiences mystical insights and knowings on a daily basis. The common, mundane nature of mystical experience is one of the best-kept secrets; its neglect and cover-up has given us a society in which we have no framework for speaking about our mystical perceptions—be it a sudden impulse or synchronicity, the urge to write a poem or song, or a vision of immense beauty. (p. 13)

She suggests that when we are distant from these dimensions of ourselves, we become unbalanced, lose touch with reality, and fall into disease and disharmony. She suggests that "most mature adults have lost the key to subtle reality, except in dreams; they are imprisoned in a cage of physical reality, doomed to walk the mundane round of existence without sparkle or soul" (Matthews, 1995, p. 22). As described by T. S. Eliot (1925):

> *Remember us— if at all— not as lost*
> *Violent souls, but only*
> *As the hollow men*
> *The stuffed men . . .*
> *This is the way the world ends*
> *This is the way the world ends*
> *This is the way the world ends*
> *Not with a bang but a whimper.*

The hollowness is evident. Today, many of us and many professions are lured into a web of seductive technologies of personal computers, electronic notebooks, palm pilots, cellular telephones, digital television, microwave ovens, and PowerPoint presentations. This quest leaves us lurching and lunging to drive the future, and force it upon ourselves. The blue haze I might have peered through as I chatted with friends over a glass of wine or a cup of coffee at a neighborhood café is no longer from dim lights and cigars, but from web surfers whose screens cast the eerie light of another world. But that other world is not an inner one, of the soul, but one premised on digitization and technology.

In my own profession of librarianship, for example, I am struck by the hum and tap of computers where I was once, long ago, entranced by the crackle of cellophane on the children's books I borrowed. Where I once listened to frogs and birds outside the library window, I now hear the scurry of cars and the impatience of jackhammers as they work to be rid of the old and get on with the new. Through conversations with academic colleagues, I am struck by their anxiety about getting the latest facts, figures and theories to relay to their students, and ensuring that lectures are now delivered via PowerPoint. Librarians aspire to be *cybrarians*. Teachers want more "meat" and less "sentiment" in learning environments. Staff relations officers want to become conversant with the current mechanics and methodologies of managing and appraising staff and measuring its productivity. Yet, I am hopeful that many, like me, remember:

> *The Book*
> *There is no Frigate like a Book*
> *To take us Lands away*
> *Nor any Courses like a Page*
> *Of prancing Poetry—*
> *This Traverse may the poorest take*
> *Without oppress of Toll—*
> *How frugal is the Chariot*
> *That bears the Human soul.*

(Emily Dickinson, n.d.)

This is not to suggest entirely that technology has no soul. I merely want to remind us of what was so eloquently expressed by John Cotton Dana, the head of the Free Public Library of Newark, New Jersey, in the early 1900s, said of books and "mere words": "we read them, we hear them—and they conquer us." I argue that soul be juxtaposed fairly within social frameworks that value and hold sacred other aspects of human reality. For inside and outside of librarianship, many long for a full, meaningful and magical life. It is encouraging to notice that in our collective longing we are today witnessing an increased interest in spirituality across North America. Bookstore shelves are well stocked with books bearing the word *soul* in the title, and eco-tourism is an emerging industry. Churches are again filling. There is a proliferation of alternative spiritual opportunities, some seeking to unite the body with the spirit. On my e-mail within the last week, I've been invited to workshops such as tantra yoga and healing voice/dancing spirit. A Saskatoon-based dance studio called The Refinery offers a course called Dancing our Divinity, which is a journey into dance as prayer and offering, as well as Arabianna belly dancing to express one's soulful sensuality.

Too, some are seeking this renewal through a heightened interest in First Nations' culture, which usually derives from a sincere and heart-felt interest to infuse greater spirituality into their lives. Matthews suggests that those without a spiritual tradition often warm themselves at others' fires, but ultimately they must return to their own hearth and make fire there (Matthews, 1995). However, I would add that, as Matthews herself notes, some of these traditions span many locations of the world and many cultures. The use of rocks, the circle and drumming, for example, are found globally throughout history (Redmond, 1997), and are there for us all to enjoy, embrace and reclaim.

I believe that the search for an understanding of the soul, and our desire to include the richness of soul in our everyday lives, will achieve more cogency in the years to come. Each culture has its own roots, songs, stories and traditional wisdom. And by inclusion, each family and person has aspects of these as well.

We are experiencing an increased quest to uncover, and perhaps create anew, these elements that add color and texture to the tapestries of our lives. Many of us are trying in our own way to make spiritual, soulful connections, and striving to make our lives more meaningful at an individual level. Some are constructing their own stories by which to live, and are not as willing to accept a prepackaged product, religion, or approach.

As we enter a new millennium, we are at a unique and pivotal time in human history. While we may continue on a path of scientism, we may also begin to entertain and explore questions of soul. We might ask what soul means, and how we might capture or recapture a sense of it and its place in our lives—within the context of our families, our communities, our institutions and our professions—and so we ask this of librarianship.

## Excavating Conceptions of Soul in Context

The Greek word for soul, *psych*, also means *butterfly*. This conjures a vision of mythical beauty, and lightness and peace—it seems an embodiment of nature itself. It represents the ability for soul to alight if we advance upon it with rigidity or with too much intent. Perhaps, as Alan Briskin (1996) suggests, we need to move in toward soul quietly and respectfully; sit close to it awhile, learn what we are able, and move in closer over time:

> If we approach it with objective reason, we risk pinning its wings to study it. And if we sentimentalize it, making it only a concept for our best intentions, then we risk it flying away from our benevolent net. To approach the soul with respect and rigor, we must be prepared to appreciate its capacity for meta-morphosis, its contradictory nature in its habit of taking flight and remaining still. We must be prepared to follow its path as it has appeared in ancient traditions and as it still appears in our day-to-day lives. (p. 12)

This suggests that we may not want to "pin the butterfly" in our attempt to explore and understand soul; we are well served to afford it a fluid nature. We can hardly say for certain what soul means today, or how it may change tomorrow. It is amorphous and dynamic. Likewise, research and writing based on such a phenomenon is best undertaken (and read) with a very open frame of mind, which also allows the ideas and suggestions to be fluid, along with the visions it conjures in the reader's mind. Such an opportunity may elicit for the reader ideas of creative application, enjoyment or moments for reflection. Soul, posits Thomas Moore (1996a), is a strange word. While we use it, and it is ever common, a definition eludes us. We have to be satisfied with descriptions, ancient and modern, that help us to meditate upon its meaning. Such a description is offered by David Elkins (1995), who suggests:

> Soul resists our Western need for operational definitions. The soul reminds us that there is another world, a world far deeper and more primordial than our logical processes. Soul is the door to this ancient imaginal world; she (Greek and Latin words for soul are both feminine nouns) is mythic and poetic in the deepest sense of these terms. To know the soul, we must lay aside our rational ways of knowing and open ourselves to the world of reverence, feeling and imagination, . . . imagery, poetry, art, ritual, ceremony, and symbol. We meet the soul when we are stirred by a person or music, moved by a poem, struck by a painting, or touched by a ceremony or symbol. Soul is the empathic resonance that vibrates within us at such moments. She is the catch of the breath, the awe in the heart, the lump in the throat, the tear in the eye. These are the signs of the soul, the markers of her presence that let us know we have touched her or she has touched us. (p. 85)

James Hillman (1989) attempts a concrete definition of soul, and suggests, ironically, that we cannot look to science to assist us. He claims that soul refers to the deepening of events into experiences; it makes possible, whether in love or in religious concern, a special relation with death; it refers to the imaginative possibilities of our natures, the experiencing through reflective speculation, dream, image and fantasy—that mode which recognizes all realities as primarily symbolic or metaphysical.

Barrett (1986) challenges us to consider the body as well as the soul, spirit and emotions. He writes: "The body we know is rarely sharply distinguishable from the soul: in our moods and feelings we are not often sure what part is physical and what not. There is no sharp dividing line between" (p. 20). He describes a psychophysical unit:

> What we call body and what we call soul are abstractions, aspects of one unitary reality and process. In our ordinary experience (which must always be our primary point of departure and return) we cannot always tell where body ends and soul begins. As our mood lifts, our body soars with it, and as our body sags, the spirit droops with it. (p. 26)

Alan Briskin supports this idea, in my view, by suggesting that while modern culture sees the body as a receptacle for the soul, it might be useful to think of the soul as embodied in us, relating to the world through the senses. "The senses by which we taste, touch, smell, see, hear and intuit are the portals by which the soul knows itself and others. The soul is not 'inside' but rather at the boundary between inner experience and outer events" (Briskin, 1996, p. 146).

Some writers such as Hillman and Elkins make distinctions between the soul and spirit. Elkins (1995), for example, distinguishes soul from spirit, and asserts that the latter has to do with height. Spirit is the phoenix rising from the ashes; soul is the ashes from which the phoenix arose. Similarly, Hillman (1989) suggests that spirit may rise above or move beyond the valley of soul, and it is escapist, literalistic, artistic, and creative. Finally, some, including Hillman, suggest that soul has to do with religion, while others, such as Elkins, say that it does not.

Further, and most importantly, the definitions of soul and the discourse concerning it include a worldview, and a concern for others. Writers such as Cousineau (1994), Sardello (1992) and Moore (1992) take great care to make clear that while each person has soul, soul is much bigger than each individual and it is an aspect of the world in its totality. Like love, it is pervasive and creates connections between all persons and communities and elements of the world. It is in the heart of our bodies, and in the canyons of the land, and in the waves that connect one star to another. In this sense, it is less a thing than a way of viewing the world, our responsibility to it, and the joy in it. Soul, in this sense, is a conjoining of all that is, and portrays how in honoring it, we may live well together.

Conceptions such as spirit, emotion, the body, and the world can all be considered closely related to soul. Here, I will generally and simply use the term *soul,* which I intend to represent a confluence of all of these interpretations or elements. *Soul* seems to more accurately reflect what I want to discuss, which is that which occurs at a very deep personal and individual level. Soul is not unlike the Northern Lights referenced in the Tribute at the beginning of this book. It is akin to a mythical dance that touches the senses and resonates at a visceral level beyond them, and sometimes leaves us standing at the edges of language, agape—uncertain even, how to define it.

Certainly, the concept of soul is an elusive and uncomfortable one for many. Particularly in a world heavily influenced by science, we are much more accustomed to dealing with that which is quantifiable, observable and tangible. Gary Zukav, a Harvard educated physicist, has himself struggled with the transition from the world of science to those beyond. He suggests this struggle has been shared with great minds and souls such as William James, Carl Jung, Benjamin Lee Whorf, Niels Bohr and Albert Einstein. Of them, Zukav (1989) claims:

> I came to understand that what motivated these men was not earthly prizes or the respect of colleagues, but that they put their souls and minds on something and reached the extraordinary place where the mind could no longer produce data of the type that they wanted, and they were in the territory of inspiration where their intuitions accelerated and they knew that there was something more than the realm of time and space and matter, something more than physical life. They knew it. They could not necessarily articulate this clearly because they were not equipped to talk about such things, but they felt it and their writing reflected it. (p. 13)

This idea has been expressed more recently by Louis Heshusius and Keith Ballard (1996) in the book *From Positivism to Interpretivism and Beyond: Tales of Transformation in Educational and Social Research*. In this work, the editors invited researchers to reflect upon their own personal transition from positivist to alternative research methodologies. The contributors recount their personal internal and external struggles to become reawakened to somatic, tacit knowledge. One contributor reflecting on all of the writers in the text summarizes the experience of the transition as the "dark night of the soul" and a "coming home" of the researchers to their true selves.

Research and writing concerned with aspects of soul encounter a number of fundamental challenges. One is the claim that it is very difficult to acquire "scientific" evidence of the relationship between soul and leadership. Hillman (1989), for example, a prominent writer about aspects of soul, speaks against positivistic approaches in favor of interpretive ones, in order to capture an understanding of the elusive realm of soul. A second challenge to writing of this nature is the difficulty in understanding, expressing in terms of language, and being willing to share experiences of such a personal nature.

I anticipated that there would be an even greater degree of difficulty in expressing aspects related to the soul. As noted earlier, this is a topic that is somewhat removed from Westernized daily interactions. In the first instance, we may not recognize our relationship to soul, be able to identify it, or even be able to articulate it. Describing what occurs at a soul level does not lend itself easily to be shared through words and texts. Some elusive aspects of our lives take us to the edges of language and there render us mute. Perhaps it is "a catch in the breath, a tear in the eye, a lump in the throat" (Elkins, 1995, p. 85) because it is difficult to express in words. Perhaps soul is more closely aligned with or related to the body than it is to the mind, where words live. Or perhaps it is not of the body, but of some other visceral place that has no locality, that has no name, other than *soul*.

An undertaking of this nature could be perceived as rather presumptuous. It presumes not only to have captured aspects of another's soul, but to have understood it in some measure as a unique phenomenon, linked and related it to other souls, and then communicated a sense of that totality in writing. Moreover, such liberties may be considered invasive; this research requires that participants reflect upon and reveal aspects of themselves and their experiences that have occurred at a very deep human level—indeed, at a soul level. While respondents had choice in the instances of such feeling that they chose to share, they were still asked that they think about deep, personal feelings.

Too, some might suggest that to research the soul is folly. But,

> to recognize that the soul of a man is unknowable, is the ultimate achievement of wisdom. The final mystery is oneself. When one has weighed the sun in the balance, and measured the steps to the moon, and mapped out the seven heavens star by star, there still remains oneself. Who can calculate the orbit of his own soul?" (Wilde, 1911, p. 119-120)

Understanding this, I was compelled to persevere. But in doing so, I am reminded that as one person trying to understand others, try as I might, I may not have always gotten it exactly right. Yet, getting it *right*, as we will come to see, is not the point of exploring soul. Ultimately, I have come to be most humbly thankful for being permitted to take the liberties and make the presumptions inherent in this rendering, and ever grateful to those who participated in this work.

# Chapter Two

# Ancient, Contemporary, Critical, Feminist and Alternative Leadership

Keith Grint (1997) observed that articles on leadership were produced at a rate of ten per day in the 1990s; at this rate, he surmised, we shall run out of wood before we can see the tree. A search for the word "leadership" in the title yielded 4,694 titles in one database. Interpretations and definitions are plentiful to be sure, and as such become an example of the adage that the more we think we know, the less we actually do know. What does seem to be the case, however, is that while leadership ultimately defies definition, it is recognized when experienced— we know it when we see it—through either the leadership of others or our own leadership experiences. Moreover, the concept of leadership is a moving target because society is continually changing.

As a component and reflection of a dynamic society, leadership is a social construction. This means that leadership is designed and determined over time by both individuals and the societies of which it is a part. Leadership occurs in all social forums such as the family, the economy, the state, work, education, religion, and leisure activities. Within those forums, and as a social construction as described by Peter Berger and Thomas Luckman in *The Social Construction of Reality*, influential humans are able, indeed required to construct and reconstruct leadership according to values we hold and esteem. The objectives and inherent definitions of leadership vary and shift as do the times and societies in which they belong and reflect.

Illumination of this claim can be attained by a cursory glance at the meaning of leadership across contemporary counties and cultures. C. Brooklyn Derr, Sylvie Roussillon and Frank Bournois edited a book entitled *Cross-Cultural Approaches to Léadership Development* that presents, compares and contrasts leadership in countries such as Germany, China, Japan, and France. In some cases they incorporate the ways in which this manifests differently for women and men in various countries. After the fall of the Third Reich in Germany and in the aftermath of World War II, many of the German people, both nationally and internationally, were questioning their culture. The result of that painful process, according to Michel Petit and Christian Scholz (in Derr, et. al., 2002) was a rejection of an elite of any sort, including a leadership elite. Business came to be built upon a spirit of professionalism and cooperation centered on research and development. Higher education is premised upon equity of access and those working within organizations that have short-term technical courses are offered opportunities to pursue higher levels of education. There is a commitment to equality of access, equality of treatment and a protection of those who are socially disadvantaged toward the greater, or common good. Organizational executives, after years of experience and training, work cooperatively with others and evolve into master craftsmen and are highly respected.

Italian style leadership, according to Luciano Traquandi and Patrizia Castellucci, is premised in many cases upon familial relationships (in Derr, et al. 2002). There are many smaller family-run businesses that are managed by owners/bosses, who are generally male. Typically, these individuals like to be in control and seek those who they can manage and groom. They will intentionally select family members who have been raised to accept family traditions.

In Japan and France, those with leadership potential are carefully selected and groomed, and the school one attends is very important. Much attention is given to the attention and selection of the elite. The role of women in these two cultures is interesting. There are few female leaders in Japan, and when they are in leadership positions, companies place on them burdens that are manageable for males, but typically not for females if they are married or have families (Derr, et al. 2002). The role and expectation of women in France, by comparison, is very different, and is also distinct from that of North American culture. In North America, we believe that there should be equality of opportunity, women can have both a career and a personal life (career comes first in leader circles), sexuality and flirtation should remain outside of the workplace, what one does outside of work impacts the workplace, and that getting a job depends on merit and market forces. French assumptions are striking in their contrast. It is assumed that individuals differ as a result of social class and educational background, women can have a career and a personal life, but motherhood is paramount and should be accommodated at work, women must use all of their resources (including their attractiveness) to have influence at work. They believe that women should be women and express themselves as they are comfortable doing, what one does outside the workplace is nobody's business, and that one should be guaranteed a job and enough income to live (a socialist orientation) (Derr, et al. 2002).

Within any given society, at any moment in time, definitions of leadership are abundant, and readily available: Nancy Huber (1998) offers a list of definitions dating back to 1921 and Rashelle Karp and Cindy Murdock (1998) offer a full bibliographic essay tracing the history of library leadership articles. Definitions of leadership evolved from those premised upon the ability of persons to influence and motivate others to work toward a common goal, toward later definitions that reflect a leaders ability to create and enhance opportunities for the self-actualization of others. Additionally, in the late 1980s, Warren Bennis introduced a distinction between the role of a manager and leader:

| **Manager:** | **Leader:** |
| --- | --- |
| Administers | Innovates |
| Is a copy | Is an original |
| Maintains | Develops |
| Focuses on systems and structures | Focuses on people |
| Relies on control | Inspires trust |
| Has a short range view | Has a long-range perspective |
| Asks how and when | Asks what and why |
| Has eye on the bottom line | Has eye on the horizon |
| Imitates | Originates |
| Accepts the status quo | Challenges the status quo |
| Is the classic good soldier | Is their own person |
| Does things right | Does the right thing |

In the above Warren Bennis provides what the sociologist Max Weber might call an ideal type. The distinctions presented between leadership and management offer an exaggeration through which we are able to recognize the differences between the two; we can more readily see what is meant by one as compared to the other by labeling what exists at the ends of a continuum. However, it must be recognized that these are elements on a continuum, and one should take care to avoid creating false dichotomies between leadership and management. There are degrees of overlap between the columns above. Further, they are not linear, but rather are interrelated and dialectical. For example, people make up structures and systems and these are empty without the people who maintain them. Therefore, both systems and structures and the people within them must be considered where they intersect or individual human beings will be forced into inappropriate structures and ultimately rebel, leaving the systems nonfunctional or collapsed.

Embracing the recognition of workers as human beings, Peter Senge offers a contemporary definition of leadership, in which he characterizes leadership as centering on the subtle and important tasks of engaging leaders as designers, stewards and teachers who are responsible for building organizations were people expand the capabilities of others to understand complexity, clarify vision and encourage continuous learning. Considering the evolution of definitions that reflect that leadership is a social construct subject to change, we might move beyond pithy definitions and examine the evolving nature of leadership within social contexts.

My own personal point of departure, and that to which I will return at the end of this chapter, is that we are all called to lead, and we are all leaders in various capacities. While some may challenge this assertion, and indeed some of my own professors within academic structures have done so, I will contend that we are all capable of leadership and called to lead when we are so moved, inclined, impassioned, when we see room for improvement, or are compelled to make a difference because we can no longer tolerate the way things are. This happens to greater and lesser degrees, in the various roles we hold, and may impact our nations, our communities, our professions, our families or simply ourselves. Similar to Germaine Greer's understanding that the personal is political, sound self-leadership is imperative to well led communities. This assumption informs my presentation of leadership styles. In offering an interpretation of some leadership styles, it is not my intention to provide a full description and critique of relevant theory; I leave that to the great many whose life work it is to explicate such ideas and refer you to that vast body of literature. One work that I would most strongly recommend is *Leadership: Classical, Contemporary and Critical Approaches* (1997) edited by Keith Grint. Drawing on Grint's work as a model, what I will offer here is a brief overview of leadership theory, supplemented by alternative leadership models and close with a brief comment on my own views and preferences regarding leadership.

## The Ancient Leadership of Sun Tzu

In the sixth century, B.C., Sun Tzu wrote *The Art of War* which has been defined as the oldest military treatise in the world and one of the earliest explications of the tenets of sound leadership (Michaelson, 2001). Some of the principles of this thinking still offer insight in today's world inside or outside of the military:

- It is best to take a state intact; to ruin it is inferior;
- To win all battles is not the acme of skill—to subdue the enemy without fighting is the acme of skill;
- First, attack the enemy's strategy;
- Next, disrupt their alliances;
- The worst policy is to attack their cities.

He offers variables of occupying ground:

- To gain ground, unite with your allies;
- You should not linger in desolate ground;
- In enclosed ground, resourcefulness is required;
- In death ground, fight;
- There are some roads not to follow, some troops not to strike, some cities not to assault;
- If contesting ground, ensure there is something to win;
- Sometimes the sovereign need not be obeyed.

Perhaps you yourself have had occasion to employ some of the foregoing techniques. Finally, Sun Tzu suggests that there are four qualities that are dangerous in the character of a general, or a leader:

- If reckless, one can be killed;
- If cowardly, captured;
- If quick tempered, made to look a fool;
- If too delicate, culminated.

## Contemporary Leadership

Some contemporary leadership models include: strong man, transactor, visionary or charismatic, superleader, and situational leader. The strong man is the John Wayne type who employs ostensible strength, skill and power, controls knowledge and rewards, may use force and has positional power. The transactor uses rational exchange where work is performed for offered rewards, the focus is on goals, and the direction and supporting wisdom reside with the leader. The visionary hero or charismatic leader is often recognized in political leaders who provide motivating visions, and lead organizations or groups through the ability to inspire and persuade. The power for these leaders is derived from the followers who are willing to support the leader and embrace his or her vision. The superleader or the transformational leader focuses on the followers and their potential contribution and shares power by unleashing the potential of the followers. This type of leader is visionary and willing to question the status quo. The situational leader employs a variety of methods to lead depending on the situation and may use techniques such as directing, coaching, supporting, delegating and mentoring.

Two additional and more recent approaches to leadership are distributed leadership and rotational leadership. Distributed leadership is that in which leadership is shared among members of a group or organization and numerous persons are responsible for different aspects of operations. Rotational leadership is that in which leadership for any single aspect of an organization's operations is rotated from one person to another on a regular basis. These two latter approaches to leadership are beneficial because various people are able to take leadership roles and thereby offer their own unique talents and ideas. Furthermore, others more typically involved in leadership positions are less likely to suffer from burnout. For this to work well, it is useful to have a shared vision and common set of organizational values, as well as sound communication structures.

# Critical and Feminist Approaches to Leadership

There is an emerging body of critical, feminist and postmodern frameworks that inform our understanding of leadership paradigms. This literature explicates the ways in which the social construct of leadership perpetuates gender and class inequity. It also reinforces learned and sanctioned inaction, and paradoxically, unveils the pressure to work and perform at greater levels than ever before.

Gary Gemmill and Judith Oakley explore leadership as an alienating social myth that preserves an existing and dysfunctional social system that perpetuates privilege as well as serves as a legitimizing tool for individual inaction and abdication of responsibility. In a convincing deconstruction of leadership, which uncovers hidden assumptions and meanings, they argue that typical leadership theory inherently claims that leaders are necessary for the functioning of organizations. This belief in hierarchy and an unequal distribution of power is an ideology that is embraced without question. First, it diverts responsibility from individuals to "the other"—in this case, the leader. We await those who will come along to fix all that is wrong, lament when they don't materialize or criticize when "they" are only marginally effective. These ill-guided expectations entrap the leaders as well as the followers, which deepens social despair and entrenches massive learned helplessness, in which individuals feel alienated and ineffective. Second, leadership theories in their attempt to explicate *trait* or *great person* concepts reinforce and reflect the widespread tendency of people to deskill themselves and idealize leaders by implying that only a select few are good enough to exercise initiative (Gemmill and Oakley, 1997). Finally, Gemmill and Oakley suggest that *empowerment* has become a magic solution to effect change. However, without an examination of the construct of leadership and the role it plays, attempts to empower others will fall short of their mark by appearing to shift responsibility to those without actual authority, and to those who remain uncertain of their skills and their potential to contribute. Such programs may also be seen as an attempt to co-opt others into believing that top management is sharing power, although structural changes are not occurring.

The pressure to lead is sometimes expanded to include the pressure to continually learn and perform at greater and greater levels within the workplace to the benefit of the organization. Tara Fenwick, for example, in *Questioning the Concept of the Learning Organization* asserts that being required to learn is critiqued as a distortion of individual interests into a tool for competitive advantage where learners are expected to learn more, learn better and learn faster. Thus, we are always in deficit.

A feminist view of leadership can be characterized in various ways, but can also be viewed as one that redefines power as the ability to influence people to act in their own interests, rather than the goals of the leader, and redistributes power to be shared among group members. It is also premised upon mutual encouragement and support, and recognition of the skills and contributions of individual members.

A patriarchal and paternalistic experience of leadership was the reality for early female library leaders. As the first female library director at McGill University, the first female director to assume the equivalent status of a dean, and the first female national librarian, Marianne Scott revolved in the circles of men. At the first dean's retreat she attended she was literally patted on the head. Reflecting upon this experience, Dr. Scott shares the hope that the new generation of female leaders can be more outspoken. By exploring dominant views of leadership and by being prepared to deconstruct and challenge them, we may well realize Dr. Scott's hope.

## Alternative Leadership

After all is said and done, we must choose. I've explored many leadership theories and come now to one which appeals above the others. It could be characterized in various ways, but I shall refer to it as alternative leadership, and draw firstly upon the writing of Christina Baldwin's *Calling the Circle*.

Baldwin speaks broadly of a new (or renewed from historic times) way of living together, making decisions and creating a sustainable, empowering and nurturing world. She argues that this is to be done through the circle, which is a "council of ordinary people who convene to accomplish a specific task and to support each other. In this circle, leadership rotates, responsibility is shared and a sense of invisible wisdom provides the cohesion of the group" (Baldwin, p. 2). Any one person, in her description, can initiate or call a circle. The group's operating principles, goals, processes, and actions are decided upon by the group. Acknowledgement of the role and place of the heart as well as the head will permit spiritual energy to be a guiding force. In this way:

> A circle is not just a meeting with the chairs rearranged. A circle is a way of doing things differently . . . it is a return to our original form of community as well as a leap forward to create a new form of community. By calling the circle, we rediscover an ancient process of consultation and communion that, for tens of thousands of years, held the community together and shaped its course. (Baldwin, p. 24)

Baldwin traces the use of circle to the campfire and the council and reminds us that it was used by the Inuits of the Arctic Circle, the Aborigines of Australia, the North American Indians, and African tribes. The symbol of the circle was also used by European cultures as evident at Stonehenge, by the pioneers of North America, and in marriage ceremonies through the use of wedding bands. Certainly, the use of the circle has been important throughout time, and across cultures.

Embedded in many views of alternative leadership are alternative concepts of power. Alan Briskin sees power:

> Not as domination of others but as the capacity to express one's inner self, one's talent, passion, and skill, as a very soulful experience. Internal power is important to the soul because without it we cannot effectively negotiate the interaction between inside and outside. Soulfulness requires both inner work—finding meaning and purpose—and outer work—seeking avenues for expression. (p. 208)

Some mistakenly think that power is coercive and rests in the ability to reward or punish. But authentic power is internal and is realized in freely striving for self-actualization. We use our power when we use our internal gifts, strengths, abilities and talents. Paradoxically, leaders gain more power when they allow others to embrace their personal power. By allowing others to recognize and use the power inherent in their individual talents, strengths, and abilities, organizations benefit from the creativity and productivity within the workplace. Such internal power cannot be given away by a supervisor, but can be only claimed—only individuals can creatively use their talents, gifts and abilities.

Max De Pree in *Leading without Power: Finding Hope in Serving Community* (1997) writes that the most successful organizations of the information age will function with individuals acting freely in dynamic ways because people will increasingly follow willingly or not at all. He examines nonprofit organizations in the United States (such as libraries) and observes the strength of such constructs which are premised upon love—love of people, one's God, or one's work—equity, truth, justice, respect, tolerance and the nurturing of others.

# Chapter Three

# Bison in the Storm:
# Leaders and Leadership Qualities

## Some with Soul: Leader Profiles

Great libraries and great librarians have existed throughout time. Ancient libraries date back to 2300 B.C. at the site of ancient Ebla, near Syria, and the start of the great libraries as we know them today can be traced to the Greeks of 1600, B.C. (Casson, 2001). Throughout time, visionary political leaders and librarians have had a large impact on the formation of libraries and of library services for the scholars and citizens. Librarians of ancient time such as Zenodotus, the Library Director at Alexandria (founded around 300 B.C.), Aristophanes of Byzantium, and Callimachus of Cyrene, to name a few, as well as more contemporary figureheads such as Melvil Dewey, S.R. Ranganathan, and Jesse Shera, have all contributed much to our profession. While we may examine historically the contributions of persons such as these, we might also consult current library leaders. It is this later approach that I have taken in this chapter.

Nine library leaders throughout Canada and the United States were invited to participate in this book. They were invited because of their reputation for leadership excellence both within libraries and outside of them, within broader community and government organizations. They were invited also because I knew them personally or knew of them through colleagues, as persons who bring energy, passion and soul to their work.

Their preferred voices and styles of writing are presented here, either in the first or third person, which serves to not only tell their stories, but to offer alternative ways of presenting themselves as leaders in terms of the familiar and the more formal. Through these descriptions, and the various approaches to them, we are offered tangible evidence that each leader is unique, and does their work, creates their magic and weaves their tales distinctly. While we know this on a cognitive level, I was struck one afternoon in the corridors of the library school when a professor said to me: "You know, Donna, you don't need to lead the same way others do." While I knew this, it was not until someone actually said this to me that I internalized the reality and began the process of finding the courage to do things my way, just as he, and each leader, has had to do. So I offer the following self-portrayals as they were sent to me, as individual literal representations of leader uniqueness as well as a collective metaphor for unique leadership that serves an entire profession. Through this, it is my intent and desire to remind us all that we ought never to feel like there is only one correct way to do things, or that there is any formula to follow, or any one way to lead, or any one way to either express or to follow your soul's desire.

## Dr. Ken Haycock
## School of Library, Archival and Information Studies
## University of British Columbia, Vancouver, Canada

Ken Haycock was born in 1948 and attended school in Hamilton and London, Ontario where he obtained his B.A. in political science from the University of Western Ontario in 1968 and Diploma of Education in 1969. He began his career as a secondary school history teacher and teacher-librarian at Glebe Collegiate Institute in Ottawa and was a department head and part of the day staff at Colonel By Secondary School in Ottawa in 1970. During this time he completed qualifications at the University of Toronto to become an Ontario specialist in school librarianship and later completed his Masters of Education in curriculum and educational foundations at the University of Ottawa. In 1972 he moved to Guelph to become educational media consultant K-13 with the Wellington County Board of Education. From 1972 to 1976 the Board renovated more than 30 school libraries, developed policies on qualifications and staffing and instituted a vigorous staff training program; he also served as a public library trustee, his local union president, established a special library, completed his A.M.L.S. at the University of Michigan through commuting 500 miles each week and was elected president of the Canadian School Library Association.

In 1976 he moved to the west coast to become coordinator for the Vancouver School Board's more than one hundred school libraries, district resource services and special libraries; in 1984 he was named acting manager of elementary/secondary education and in 1985 became a member of Vancouver's senior management team, responsible for curriculum and program development and implementation, curriculum resources and technologies and staff development for 7,000 employees at 115 sites. During this time he was also principal of a large elementary school and completed his doctorate in educational leadership at Brigham Young University in Utah.

In 1992 he returned to librarianship as a tenured professor and director of the School of Library, Archival and Information Studies at the University of British Columbia on a five year contract; in 1997 he accepted a five year reappointment. In 2002 he chose to move to full-time research, teaching and service as a faculty member.

Ken Haycock's areas of special interest and accomplishments are education for library and information studies, organizational leadership and development, implementation of change and staff development, and teacher-librarianship. He has held research grants recently for the study of the characteristics of directors of large urban public libraries and of branch managers, staff development, youth services in public libraries, and the effectiveness of the teacher-librarian. Ken presents papers and leads workshops at innumerable conferences of educators, librarians and managers, particularly in the areas of leadership, quality management, advocacy, organizational effectiveness, translating research into practice and collaborative planning for information literacy. In 2000 he delivered a paper on the education of university and research librarians at the annual conference of the International Federation of Library

Associations and Institutions [IFLA] in Jerusalem where he was elected chair of the Section on Education and Training.

Dr. Haycock has been an active and contributing member of the library profession since 1969. In 1974 he became the youngest president of the Canadian School Library Association and in 1977 the youngest president of the Canadian Library Association; he introduced a number of innovations that have been institutionalized, and increased membership in both cases. He has also served as a public library trustee and elected school board chair. Ken is an active member of more than thirty professional associations. He has served on more than two dozen government and community boards as diverse as federal publishing juries, community information, elimination of sexism, race relations and community services. He is a member of the American Library Association's Council and its Executive Board. He was elected city councillor in West Vancouver in 1999. Ken is past president of the American Association of School Librarians and of the Council for Canadian Learning Resources where he established Resource•Links: Connecting Classrooms, Libraries and Canadian Learning Resources; he is also immediate past executive director of the International Association of School Librarianship and edits *Teacher Librarian: The Journal for School Library Professionals*.

At the University of British Columbia, Ken chaired the Graduate Council's New Programs and Curriculum Committee and served on committees of the Senate, on the Faculty of Arts' Strategic Planning Committee and the Graduate Studies Committee on Equity in Political Science.

Ken has received Distinguished Service Awards from the American Association of School Librarians, the British Columbia Teacher-Librarians' Association, the Canadian Library Association and the Canadian School Library Association, the first Grolier Award for Research and the Distinguished School Administrator Award from the Canadian School Library Association. He was named by Phi Delta Kappa, an international honor society, as one of the leading young educators in North America (one of three in Canada) and received the Queen Elizabeth II Silver Jubilee Medal from the

Governor-General for contributions to Canadian society. He is a Fellow of the Canadian College of Teachers (one of ten) and an Honorary Life Member of the Canadian Library Association. In 2001 he was awarded the Herbert and Virginia White Award by the ALA for advocacy and promotion of the profession of librarianship.

Ken enjoys research and writing—with more than one hundred books, chapters, articles and research papers. Ken works with a graduate student each year to produce "Trends and issues in library and information services in Canada" for the *Bowker Annual: Library and Book Trade Almanac*; he works collaboratively with students on research projects, one of which was a comprehensive review of search engines, subject directories and portals for young people published by Neal-Schuman. He is a committed and passionate advocate for libraries and librarians.


**Dr. Scott Bennett**
**University Librarian, Yale University**
**New Haven, Connecticut, United States**

I was born in 1939 in Kansas City, Kansas. My father was a self-taught soils engineer who worked as a civilian for the Army Corp of Engineers building earth dams on the Missouri River and elsewhere. Toward the end of a most successful career, he developed a private consulting practice that took him many places worldwide. My mother was a homemaker and a bowling instructor. I have two sisters.

I was raised in Omaha, Nebraska. I was a troublemaker and a poor student in grade school. While I had a lively imagination, I did not begin reading until the momentous discovery of *Huckleberry Finn* on the shelves of my grade school library. Thereafter I read voraciously and became a serious student, finishing high school in three years. Though my parents had not attended college, there never was a question that my sisters and I would. I graduated from Oberlin College *magna cum laude* in 1960 and went directly on to graduate studies in English literature at Indiana University, starting as a Woodrow Wilson Fellow and earning a Ph.D. in 1967.

I met my wife, Carol Jean Glass, at Oberlin. We married in 1960, had had four children and cared for a number of foster children from time to time.

I began my teaching career in 1967 in the English Department at the University of Illinois at Urbana-Champaign (UIUC), though I had taught one year as a Woodrow Wilson Teaching Intern at St. Paul's College in Lawrenceville, Virginia, in 1964-1965. I had mixed success as a teacher and was not granted tenure in the UIUC English department. Thanks to the intervention of my department head, I moved to the University of Illinois Library in 1974 to take up editorial and fundraising duties there as well as some special collections activities. I earned a graduate library degree from UIUC in 1976. At the UIUC Library I had a number of shifting, irregular assignments, often involved with organizational change, until I left to become Associate University Librarian for Collection Development at the Northwestern University Library in 1981. There, I lead the effort to create a Preservation Department. I became the Director of the Milton S. Eisenhower Library at Johns Hopkins University in 1989 where I was instrumental in creating Project Muse at the JHU Press. In 1994, I became the University Librarian at Yale where I oversaw $60 million worth of library renovations, new construction, and space planning. I retired in 2001, although I continue to do some project work for the Council of Independent Colleges and the Council on Library and Information Resources.

I was an active research scholar until the early 1980s and had an American Council of Learned Societies Fellowship that helped to support a sabbatical leave in 1978-1979. Since the 1980s, my writing has been primarily about libraries. I have published many articles, reviews, and edited a number of books. I was an active member of the American Association of University Professors through the mid-1980s, holding local, state, and nationally elected positions. I was active in the Association of Research Libraries throughout the 1990s.

Having retired in 2001, I returned to Urbana, Illinois, where my wife and I have maintained our home since 1968. Here I enjoy my family, read voraciously, exercise my carpentry skills, enjoy our tandem kayak, take advantage of the rich musical and theatrical life of the University of Illinois, play the recorder, think about resuming my research on nineteenth century publishing history, hike when I can, and occasionally do library consulting.

## Ms. Josephine Bryant
## City Librarian, Toronto Public Library
## Toronto, Ontario, Canada

I started out quite young, but grew older with time. It all began in 1947 in a small town outside of Toronto, Canada. We were a large family. There were girls everywhere. I was the sixth of eight daughters—no boys. I bet none of you could do that if you tried. As you might guess, we were Roman Catholic. (At least my mother was. My father took an oath to be, and if the size of my family is any indication, he kept that oath to the best of his ability.) Much of the rest of my life at this time was dominated by females as well. I was educated in separate schools run by nuns in a very authoritarian tradition.

Being number six in a large family of women taught me that I would be largely responsible to provide for myself unless I was going to get married, stay at home and have babies. Eventually, I married, not once but twice, and my decision to have children was deferred at some length until my career path was established. I am the mother of two boys, David, aged 22, and Michael, 18, and step-mother to Susan, 30, and Bill, 32.

Perhaps not surprisingly, I ended up in a female-dominated profession—a very comfortable place for me. You might think that my career decision was made early and that I was knocking people out of the way to get into library school. That's not so. In fact, my decision was made like many career decisions are made. Two months before the end of my undergrad career I was swatted by the great-outstretched palm of reality asking, "And

what are you going to do now?" First, I latched onto the idea of
being a lawyer. That was a respected career. And it meant more
school. That was good. I applied, and I even got in.

Then, one evening at a party, someone mentioned library
school. I didn't know there was such a thing. But I'd always
liked libraries, and perhaps for that reason, the idea stuck. It
even meant I could continue my education at the same
university. What more could a student want? So I did it.

Thus my childhood and the first stage of my schooling ended.
In most ways, my life was very ordinary. So ordinary, in fact,
that little Joey Bryant even got a walk-on part in Ken Dryden's
book, *The Moved and the Shaken*, the story of the life of a very
ordinary man. Really. You could look it up. A supporting role in
a book about the epitome of ordinariness: how's that for
ordinary? Next thing I knew, I was working as a corporate
librarian for Ontario Hydro. For four years I did that. I was still
pretty hooked on the school thing and trying to advance my
library schooling part time. The problem with Hydro was that I
wanted to advance, but people were sitting on my head and there
was no place to go. So, in 1974, I left and finished my Master of
Library Science degree. I moonlighted as a cocktail waitress to
help see me through.

Back in those days, corporate libraries were Nowhereville.
Public libraries were the place to be. It's quite different today,
but back then, I saw my future in public libraries. So, I headed
for Brampton, Ontario, a Toronto suburb, where in 1974, I
started in the public library as Supervisor of Information
Services. It was nothing like the large public library I work for
now, but I managed to work my way up to Deputy Director and
Branch Head, a position which gave me a chance to work with
the public while at the same time having a hand in the operation
of the organization. My tasks were as varied as directing the
public service staff, budgeting and sitting on a management
committee that negotiated contracts with the library union.

Well, all this library work seemed to equip me perfectly, I
thought, to leave the library after five years and become the
owner and operator of a fitness business. The truth is, I'd always
wanted to have my own business. I wasn't going to move up any

more in Brampton, and when the opportunity arose to have my own start-up, I dove in head first, eyes closed. You may think that was an ill-advised move, and maybe it was. But those were different times back in 1979. The dinosaurs had recently died out, and, unlike today, it was a good time for taking business risks. I'm glad I did it, because it gave me a sound appreciation of what it means to run a small business. But practically speaking, it was a three-year detour that taught me it is difficult to make money in a small business.

By 1982, I was ready to head back into libraries. So I picked, and managed to get into North York Public Library, the second largest urban public library in Canada and one with a nation-wide reputation for excellence and innovation. I began in a management position similar to that which I'd left at Brampton—Area Manager. Shortly after this, I attended a public administration in local government course that provided me with an invaluable framework from which to advance my career and to view public library service as a part of the overall delivery of municipal government services. I felt ready, then, when in 1988, I was appointed Director, or Chief Executive Officer of the North York Public Library.

In 1998, the new City of Toronto and the new Toronto Public Library Board were established, incorporating six former area municipalities and the regional governments of metropolitan Toronto. Competing for the job of City Librarian for the amalgamated public library system in Toronto was a challenge, and one I'm glad to be able to say I was successful in. The real challenge came after I got the job. Running the largest public library system in Canada is a huge challenge, but, as with every great challenge, the rewards are more than worth the effort.

What else goes on in my life? I used to love tennis, but that passion has been replaced by golf, which I appreciate more as a family activity, as the ultimate head game and a great metaphor for life. As you might expect, I love to read, and have organized a book club. I enjoy jazz and opera. These passions and my family life have been important in sustaining me over the past couple of years.

## Mr. Ernie Ingles, F.R.S.C.
## Vice Provost and Chief Librarian, University of Alberta, Edmonton, Alberta, Canada

Mr. Ernie is Associate Vice President (Learning Services) at the University of Alberta. Within this context he has responsibilities for the University of Alberta Libraries, Museums and Collections Services, the University of Alberta Archives and Records Management, the Bookstore, Printing and Duplicating Services, the University of Alberta Press, University Design Inc., and a variety of services focused on the external community that comprise a business unit of University Information Enterprises. He is also responsible for administering freedom of information and protection of privacy and copyright administration.

Ernie received his Bachelor of Arts and Master of Arts degrees in history and the history of agricultural technology at the University of Calgary. He was the recipient of the Ruth Cameron Medal in 1974 upon his graduation from the School of Librarianship at the University of British Columbia. He began his career working at the University of British Columbia as a Reference Librarian, but returned after a short time to the University of Calgary where he was Head of the Department of Rare Books and Special Collections.

In the wake of the post-Expo '67 renaissance within Canada, Ernie took a personal and professional interest in the area of Canadian Studies and by the mid-1970s he was involved in a number of adventures that incrementally increased the profile of Canadian Studies within academic environments. For example, while at the University of Calgary, he was instrumental in establishing the Canadian author manuscript collections, and the Canadian architectural archives, both of which have achieved national prominence.

As a Canadianist, Ernie worked with the group that created the Canadian Institute for Historical Microreproductions (CIHM) as the founding Executive Director and Chief Executive Officer. CIHM began in 1977 with a $2,000,000 grant from the Canada Council and was charged with the responsibility of preserving and making available for research the national literature of Canada, initially through the use of archival microforms, and more recently through digital resources. By way of his involvement Ernie was able to assure the viability of the Institute, which continues to reproduce and provide access to hundreds of thousands of historical printed works.

By the mid-1980s, while remaining on the Board of Directors of CIHM, Ernie elected to return to the academic mainstream, and assumed the position as University Librarian at the University of Regina. Here he was instrumental in a number of innovations, such as his founding of the RegLIN consortium, a group of libraries working together to share an automated library system.

In 1990 he moved to the University of Alberta, where as Chief Librarian and Director of Libraries he achieved some prominence for his strategic planning initiatives, his technology planning, the creation of the NEOS consortium, the development of the province-wide Health Knowledge Network (HKN), the planning and building of a Canadian university's first remote storage and document supply facility (known as BARD: Book and Record Depository), and his award-winning outsourcing, cost-containment initiatives in partnership with Information Systems Management (ISM). In 1995, he assumed the role of Associate Vice President (Learning Systems), a new position at the university, created to provide leadership, and a framework for planning and coordinating information and instructional technology and related resources for the institution, and recently was promoted to Vice Provost and Chief Librarian.

Ernie has been an active player within the Canadian library and information technology communities, having served over one hundred professional, association, and community organizations. He has held numerous executive positions on boards, including    President of the Canadian Library Association, the Bibliographic Society of Canada, the Council of Prairie and Pacific University Libraries, and the Saskatchewan Library Association; and he has either served on, or chaired, numerous others, such as the Library Association of Alberta Executive, the Association of Library Boards of Ontario,

UTLAS International Canada, OCLC Research Libraries Advisory Board, Canadian Association of College and University Libraries, the Canadian Association of Research Libraries, the Canadian Government Publishing Centre, the Book and Periodical Development Council, the National Library of Canada, the National Research Council of Canada, the Canada Institute for Scientific and Technical Information, Statistics Canada, CANARIE, the Edmonton Freenet, TELUS, HPC Inc., the Canadian Initiative on Digital Libraries and WurcNet (now NETERA Alliance), and PeopleSoft. In addition, he has been involved in numerous arts and cultural organizations.

Ernie has published frequently, including over twenty articles or contributions, and three major monographic compilations, including his seminal reference tool the Bibliography of Canadian Bibliographies/Bibliographie des bibliographies canadiennes (Toronto: University of Toronto Press, 1994). He is a requested speaker having given well over 130 papers or presentations.

A key contribution to the Canadian library community was his founding of the Northern Exposure to Leadership Institute, now acclaimed worldwide as a landmark contribution to librarianship and professional development (and featured in chapter four of this book).

Mr. Ingles has been the recipient of numerous awards, including the Rutherford Cameron Medal for Librarianship, the Marie Tremaine Medal for Bibliography, the Canadian Association of College and University Libraries Award for Outstanding Librarian, the Innovation Achievement Award from the Canadian Association of College and University Libraries, the President's Award for Outstanding Service from the Library Association of Alberta, and Outstanding Alumni award from the University of British Columbia, School of Library, Archival and Information Science, Innovator of the Year, and Hall of Fame Inductee award sponsored jointly by Canadian Business, the Royal Bank, the Canadian Information Processing Society and the Information Technology Association of Canada, and the Outstanding Service to Librarianship Award from the Canadian

Library Association. He is also an Honorary Life Member of The Alberta Library and in 2001 he was elected as a Fellow of the Royal Society of Canada. Under this leadership the University of Alberta has been honored with five awards from the Canadian Association of University Business Officers: 1993 Quality and Productivity Award—Book and Record Depository; 1995 Quality and Productivity Award—Technical Services Outsourcing; 1996-1997 Western Regional Award—The Digital Library; and 2000 Quality and productivity Award—University of Alberta/TELUS Alliance; 2001 Quality and Productivity Award—Quality Color on Campus. In addition, his awards include the Canadian Information Productivity Award, the GIGA Gold Award for Excellence in the Application of Information Technology, and the Canadian Library Association/*Information Today* Award for Innovative Use and Application of Technology.

## Dr. Marianne Scott
## Former National Librarian, National Library of Canada, Ottawa, Ontario, Canada

Dr. Marianne Scott received her Bachelor of Arts from McGill University in Montreal, Quebec in 1949, and subsequently her Bachelor of Library Science in 1952. Upon graduation, she worked as the Law Librarian, McGill University from 1955-1974; Director of Libraries at McGill from 1975-1984, and finally, as the National Librarian of Canada from 1984 until she retired in 1999.

Dr. Scott has received numerous awards including the prestigious Officer of the Order of Canada in 1995, the Queen's Silver Jubilee Medal, the Queen's Golden Jubilee Medal, the IFLA Medal, the IFLA Honorary Fellow and honorary doctoral degrees from York University, Dalhousie University and Laurentian University.

Throughout her career, Dr. Scott has been involved with many organizations in Canada, the United States and internationally. Some of these include: International Federation of Library Associations (IFLA), International Association of Law Libraries, Association of Research Libraries, Canadian Library Association, Canadian Writer's Foundation, UNESCO, and the Centre for Research Libraries. She is also widely published, having written over thirty articles.

## *On a personal note, Marianne writes:*

An only child of the depression years, I was raised in a single parent family by a mother who encouraged me to be independent. As I grew older she also insisted that I have the potential for a "career," which was not the norm for girls in those days.

At McGill University I was just an average student, perhaps because I had no real focus. The University was swamped with returning World War II veterans so it was a very interesting and somewhat chaotic campus. Because of the lack of focus I had a great deal of difficulty finding a job after graduation—I was either underqualified or overqualified. This trauma remained with me in later years and I rarely hesitated to hire someone who really needed the experience but was overqualified for the job. When I finally did find a job, I hated the work with a passion. When the light finally went on and I applied for and was accepted into Library School, I was thrilled. This is probably the reason that I was one of the few people I knew at the time who really enjoyed the course!

My first job after graduation was not the most exciting, but for a new graduate it was the best paying job in Montreal, Quebec in May 1952 and I was in great need of money. As the second in charge in a very active special library and the only professional librarian, I was jack of all trades which provided me with a great opportunity to learn.

Three years later the offer to become the Law Librarian at McGill University was a scary challenge—I was to be in charge. I knew nothing about law and the session was already one month underway when I arrived. That I had a lot to learn is a major understatement, but with the support of colleagues at the University and new friends made through the American

Association of Law Libraries and later the Canadian Association of Law Libraries, I succeeded.

It was at this time that I really began to understand the power of Associations and started to be heavily involved—first within McGill, then provincially and of course in the two law library associations.

I was very happy and contented at the Law Library and it was with some sadness and trepidation that I left an environment I knew, where I was secure in my working knowledge and supported by friends and colleagues, to become Director of Libraries at McGill University in Montreal. However, there were several reasons for doing this, including the well-known concept of putting your money where your mouth is.

As Director of Libraries, I became more involved with national issues and had the pleasure to serve as President of the Canadian Library Association. In 1984, when I was invited to become National Librarian, I felt greatly honored as well as challenged. In this position there was more opportunity to understand the situation of libraries across Canada and also to become more involved with international librarianship, to say nothing of trying to learn about government bureaucracy.

Throughout my career I have believed in the strength of collectivity and benefited greatly from the support, the warmth and friendship received through association work.

All of this required full days and long weeks, which left little time for personal socializing. However, whenever the opportunity presented itself I found it quite easy to block out work and relax, which often involved fiddling around the house, in the garden or looking after my four-footed friends.

**Mr. James G. Neal**
**Vice President, Information Services and University Librarian, Columbia University, New York, United States**

Mr. James Neal is the Vice President for Information Services and University Librarian at Columbia University, providing leadership for university academic computing and network services and a system of 22 libraries. He also works with the Electronic Publishing Initiative at Columbia (EPIC), the Center for Research in Information Access (CRIA), the Columbia Center for New Media Teaching and Learning (CCNMTL), and serves on key academic, technology and budget policy and planning groups. Previously, he served as Dean of University Libraries at Indiana University and Johns Hopkins University, and held administrative positions in the libraries at Penn State, Notre Dame, and the City University of New York. At Columbia, Johns Hopkins, and Indiana, he has focused on digital library/electronic resource program development, library building construction and renovation projects, and fundraising and grants activities.

James has served on the Council and Executive Board of the American Library Association, on the Board and as President of the Association of Research Libraries, and as chair of OCLC's Research Library Advisory Council, as well as on numerous international, national and state professional committees. He was a member of the Organizing Committee for the International Federation of Library Associations conference in Boston in 2001 and coordinated its resource development program. He has worked on the editorial boards of journals in the field of academic librarianship. He is a member of the Board of Directors of Community of Science and the corporate advisory board of Docutek.

James is a frequent speaker at national and international conferences, consultant and published researcher with a focus in the areas of scholarly communication, intellectual property, digital library development, organizational change, human resources development, and library fundraising. He has served on the Board of Project Muse, the electronic journal publishing program at Hopkins, on the Advisory Board for the E-History Book Project at the American Council of Learned Societies, on the Advisory Board of PubMed Central at the National Institutes of Health, on the Scholarly Communication Committees of ARL and ACRL, and as chair of the Steering Committee of SPARC, the Scholarly Publishing and Academic Resources Coalition. He has represented the American library community in testimony on copyright matters before Congressional committees and was an advisor to the U.S. delegation at the World Intellectual Property Organization (WIPO) diplomatic conference on copyright. He has worked on copyright policy and advisory groups for universities and professional associations. He was selected the 1997 Academic/Research Librarian of the Year by ALA's Association of College and Research Libraries, and was recently appointed to the National Information Standards Organization (NISO).

### *On a personal note, James writes:*

After my undergraduate years at Rutgers as a Russian Studies major, I knew that my life would be spent in the academic community. I proceeded to Columbia to study at the Russian Institute and to pursue a doctorate in Russian history. After two years of study and the prospect of several years of research in Leningrad, and with a young family needing more time and support, I knew that a change in career plans was essential. In the late fall of 1971, I discovered the graduate school of library service on the upper floors of the Butler Library at Columbia, and within a year, I was working as a librarian in my first professional assignment. It certainly beat the supermarket jobs I had maintained for ten years as a student to just pay the bills. My first librarian assignment was at a community college with limited opportunities for administrative advancement and professional growth, so I almost immediately began work on a doctorate in library science at Columbia. The financial collapse of New York City in 1976 and massive budget cuts at City University took away this job but enabled a move to my first administrative assignment in an academic research library at Notre Dame. I quickly realized that I was on a path to administrative and professional leadership in academic librarianship.

I was the kid who was elected 'most likely to succeed' and 'most popular' and 'friendliest' in junior high school. I was the high school student who got involved in every student activity while also maintaining a paper route and working part-time in a supermarket. I was the part-time clerk who was advanced every summer into temporary management assignments. I was the young librarian who participated in an early academic library management intern program at Penn State. Leadership in the library, on the campus, and in the profession has consistently been part of my personal vision and commitment.

For me, leadership takes many forms: breadth of administrative responsibility, professional influence and impact, bravery in the face of ethical and political challenges, for example. My career as a librarian has embraced these elements. Leadership is innovation combined with decisive action. Leadership is knowing when to take risks, when to compete, and when to collaborate. Leadership is facilitating a team to achieve individual and shared goals. Leadership is connections, transformations, and entrepreneurship. I am a passionate librarian who believes that high quality and innovative librarianship translates into high quality learning and research in an academic community.

I think more frequently about retirement now, not about the withdrawal from professional leadership, but about the freedom to think and speak openly, to not have a day dominated by constant meetings, to be reflective and thoughtful, to be flexible and spontaneous, to be creative, to return to my academic roots.

## Mr. Stephen Abram
## Vice President of Innovation, Sirsi Corporation
## Toronto, Ontario, Canada

When Mr. Abram joined Sirsi in March of 2004, he was described as "a leading international librarian and lighthouse thinker in the North American library community." He is that; Stephen is responsible for trend forecasting, new product conceptualization and market development. Sirsi Corporation is a strategic technology partner to more than 10,000 libraries globally and is well recognized as a leading and innovative solutions creator.

Mr. Abram was previously Vice President for corporate development for Micromedia ProQuest. Stephen has been Publisher of Electronic Information for Carswell and Thomson Electronic Publishing in Canada and the United States, creating some of the leading legal information-finding tools in North America in CD-ROM, online, and web formats. He has managed libraries, marketing and information resources for Hay Management Consultants, Coopers & Lybrand (now PriceWaterhouseCoopers) as well as held positions with the Canadian law firm Smith, Lyons, Torrance, Stevenson, & Mayer, and Suncor.

Stephen has received numerous awards and honors including: The John Cotton Dana Award from the Special Libraries Association in 2003; *Library Journal's* Top 50 Librarians Shaping the Future of Librarianship 2002; Information Highways 2001 Canadian Product of the Year; Canadian Special Librarian of the Year (CASLIS/CLA) in 1998; Canadian Online Product Award in 1997; Fellow, Special Libraries Association in 1995; Mecklermedia/Internet World Canada—Best Business Web Site in 1998; and from the Information Industry Association, 1992 New Product Achievement.

Like most library leaders, Stephen has been involved in many professional activities including: Guest Editor, *Feliciter*; Ontario Library Association Vice President, 2002 President, past President; *Internet World Canada*, Editorial Board, *Computers in Libraries*; many roles with Special Libraries Association, including serving on the international board of directors for SLA; Chair, Information Industries Committee; Information Technology Association of Canada; Instructor, University of Toronto, Faculty of Information Studies; and President of the Canadian Library Association, 2004.

### *On a personal note, Stephen writes:*
I was born in the 1950s when things were much simpler—or so we think. As I grew up I watched television dominate as the communication medium. Beloved theaters in my neighborhood closed. We watched old black and white movies on TV. I was a TV junkie and rushed home to watch *I Love Lucy* for lunch daily —repeat after repeat. Along came videotapes and we could

watch color movies on TV. People predicted the end of theaters again.

I'm a born and bred Torontonian, which makes me rare in Toronto. I love the cultural and ethnic diversity of the place and the dynamism in the stirring of the cultural mélange in Canada's largest city. I'm a very urban person and get the vapors going to the country where there is no concrete beneath my feet. I love living in the center of the city. I feel safe where there are people and they're not cloistered in their houses behind their manicured green moats. I love the fact that my kids are streetwise.

While I did my Bachelor of Arts full time, I worked as a combination hardware and furniture designer for a store in a large suburban mall. It was a lot more fun and creative than you might think. Designing things like furniture and spaces is still a hobby. I did my undergraduate degree in anthropology and archaeology because I wanted to understand how humans dealt with their environment. I still do. To this day I can see how the courses I took in primitive tool design affect my approach to interface design. I can see how following the social anthropology of preliterate societies has informed my interest in knowledge management and the importance of story telling. I am concerned about how technology impacts social and knowledge ecology.

My wife, Stephanie, finished her Bachelor of Education and then put me through my Masters of Library Science. The library school made me sign a contract that I wouldn't work full time when I did my MLS. I guess they feared I might be successful at both and they would be at a loss to explain the program's rigor. I loved library school—it was the first time in my life where I felt part of something big enough to make a difference in society and broad enough for me to find a home for my wide diversity of interests. I made lifelong friends there and, indeed, I've met most of my closest friends in my work as a librarian.

I started out in business libraries. If there was one thing working retail taught me, it was that, selfishly, I didn't want to stand all day, work with the general public or cope with shift work. I worked contract first at an oil company and then I lucked into a great job with the old Currie Coopers & Lybrand consulting and accounting firm. I was their first professional librarian and they didn't really know what they wanted or needed so I got the chance to create it. Online was just arriving, microforms were still reasonably new, and I also had records management responsibilities right from the start. I learned a lot and made a lot of mistakes, from which I learned more. I did a lot of hands-on research and learned the basics.

This was, however, during the 1980's recession and they didn't raise my salary as quickly as I felt was right, so I took another position, and didn't refuse the 50 percent raise to start a new library in another international consulting firm. In this job I learned how to build a library from scratch but, more importantly, when that was done, I learned how to run a business step-by-step through taking on any role that was offered. I managed the move of the company and won a major office design award. I assumed responsibility for graphics, marketing, article publishing, firm administration, and I learned much about office management, finance, accounting, human resources, job evaluation, and hiring. It was an intense learning experience. I did, however, go through six presidents in five years, under which circumstances I was bound to find one that hated me and number six was my Waterloo.

After he fired me, I found work the next day at a law firm on contract. I'd never worked in the law before, so I found it very interesting and educational. I was only there five months but it led to my next position. I decided that I needed to change tracks and I thought that I'd like to try working in the publishing sector. Through professional friends and contacts, I was hired in an exciting new start up for the legal publishing division of Thomson internationally. They saw value in my library, business, law, tax, and searching experience. I started out as a senior product manager for an online tax service. Over time, I became a publisher and took on the early development of some of the first online and CD-ROM law products in North America. We got to create and innovate on a grand scale.

It was, however, exhausting. Being responsible for putting out 20-40 new electronic products annually required 12-hour days, 6 days a week. I had a young family and they were starting to call me "Daddy Who?" especially since the office required three hours of daily commuting. Also, the law market is very demanding and resistant to change, which can wear you down after a while. Lastly, we were tasked with being change agents for a traditional print publishing company to assist them in their evolution to an electronic publisher. So I changed jobs and went to work for Micromedia. I enjoyed the library market focus and the sheer Canadian atmosphere of the place. I also got a tiny stake in the company.

Over the years I've learned a great deal. I enjoy writing about what I've learned. I enjoy giving workshops and speeches and I have had the opportunity to give a lot around the world in the past few years. I have some good coaches and mentors and I like being a mentor or coach for others.

So now we're looking at e-Books and the long-predicted demise of print. We're struggling with what the library and information universe of the future will look like. I think back to the 1950s and the threatened demise of movies. Movies just had their highest sales year in history and they're building *huge* theaters all over Toronto. What's it all mean? I don't know. What's next for me? I don't know. As long as I can keep learning and still practice the art of librarianship in a multitude of ways and environments, then I'll be happy.


**Ms. Vivienne Monty**
**Senior Librarian, York University**
**Toronto, Ontario, Canada**

Vivienne Monty was born in Budapest, Hungary, and was brought to Canada by her parents in 1956. They settled in Toronto, where she attended private school. Starting in 1963, she commuted between Lausanne, Switzerland and home, completing her high school in both places.

She went to University of Toronto where she completed an honors Bachelor of Arts degree in History and then an Masters of Library Science. Meanwhile, she had finished a certificate in *langue et litérature française* in Lausanne. During these years,

Vivienne worked on vacations and in the evenings for her father who had his own manufacturing company.

Her first day job was where she still works today at York University. The job has varied over the years. She was first the Assistant Head of the Government Documents Library. That library absorbed the business collection within a few months of her arrival. In 1982, she was appointed the Head of the Business and Government Library, which entailed all responsibility for staff and collections. Wanderlust eventually struck and in 1987, she spent a year at the Frost Library (a bilingual campus) to fill in for a librarian on sabbatical. The next four years were spent as Internet Coordinator for the Libraries, and she is now at the Bibliothèque Frost Library, from where she finds opportunities to lead from the middle.

Over the years, she became an association junkie and activist, where her interests spread to university affairs. She has been very involved at York with the Faculty Association, and was the first librarian negotiator, as well as Treasurer, Vice President (internal), and Vice President (external).

Viviehne has a deep concern for access to government information and to solid business data. She has worked with the Government of Canada Depository Services Program to help provide access to government information in print and electronic formats.

She has been the President of the Toronto Chapter of Canadian Association Special Libraries and Information Services (CASLIS), President of CASLIS National, and Treasurer and President of the Canadian Library Assoication. She made accreditation visits for the committee on Accreditation of the American Library Association and was the Canadian member on that Committee. She was elected president of the Toronto Chapter of the Special Libraries Association (SLA), helped organize two Canadian conferences for SLA, and been involved with the Ontario Library Association and the Canadian Association of University Teachers.

She has also written seven books, two book chapters, dozens of articles, and two major indexes on CD. Vivienne has given many talks on government and business at library gatherings and conferences. She has her own small business as well, which has nothing to do with libraries and helps her keep balance in her life.


## Ms. Bridget Later Lamont
## Director of Policy Development, Office of the Governor
## Springfield, Illinois, United States

Bridget Later Lamont was named the Director of the Illinois State Library, a division of the Office of the Illinois Secretary of State, in June 1983, where she managed a staff of 109 with a budget of $63 million. The Illinois State Library had two major functions: 1) to serve as a research library for government, and 2) to coordinate and promote library development through a single state wide cooperative library network, ILLINET (Illinois Library and Information Network). Over 2,500 Illinois public and private libraries are members of the network that promotes sharing of library materials and human resources.

Major programs of the agency include annual state grants to school and public libraries for local library programs; the Illinois literacy program a statewide cooperative collection development program; automated systems and networking; and library system development. Ms. Lamont has overseen the library phases of the construction of a new 160,000 square-foot Illinois State Library building, which was dedicated in June 1990. She has been involved in the development and implementation of the Live and Learn program.

Ms. Lamont began her library career as a shelver in the Children's Department of the Wilmette Public Library and continued her work with children's library programs in the Evanston and Champaign Public Libraries. After joining the staff of the Illinois State Library in 1972, Ms. Lamont worked in the library Development Group as a professional assistant and was promoted as a library consultant specializing in children's services, and later in library systems and multitype library cooperation. She was appointed Associate Director for Library

Development in 1979; Deputy Director in 1981 and she was named Director of the Illinois State Library in 1983.

A native of Wilmette, Illinois, and the oldest of seven children, Ms. Lamont attended Regina Dominican High School in Wilmette and received her Bachelor of Arts in 1970 from Clarke College in Dubuque, Iowa. She received her Masters of Science from the University of Illinois-Urbana/Champaign in 1972.

She has served as President of the Association of Specialized and Cooperative Library Agencies, a division of the American Library Association and in 1990 won that group's Exceptional Achievement Award. Also in 1990, she was awarded the Illinois Humanities Council—Public Humanities Award and Illinois School Library Media Association Special Award. In 1991, she received the Illinois Library Association's Librarian of the Year award. She was a member of the Board of Directors of the Illinois Center for the Book and Sangamon State University Advisory Committee. Ms. Lamont resides in Springfield, Illinois with Thomas R. Lamont, partner in the law firm of Gordon and Glickson, and two sons.

## Their Lives Touched My Own

Leaders, at their best, touch the lives of the individuals with whom they work. By way of illustration, I will briefly share how each of these persons profiled here inspired me in my work or in my life, and in doing so, touched my soul. Perhaps as you read this you will call to mind the leaders you have known, and recall how they inspired and motivated you, and changed your life. Perhaps too, you will recall being frustrated and exhausted; let us together not be dismayed, reminding ourselves that what doesn't kill us makes us stronger.

For my part, among the leaders profiled here is Mr. Ernie Ingles, my first supervisor and boss, who inspires much in many and as his profile shows continues to have a career that few could maintain let alone grow with such brilliance and energy. For many in Canada, Ernie has, as another colleague once phrased it, shown us that we can live expanded versions of ourselves. We have been pushed to our limits by Mr. Ingles, and at those edges we have found more of who we are and that of which we are capable. For me, he has done this by assuming various roles: mentor, supervisor, colleague, teacher, student, co-learner, and always a very good and dear friend. Recognizing my inherent shyness as a characteristic he also possessed, he told me that a burning light cannot live under a bushel basket, that I had wisdom and intelligence, energy and insight, and in this inspired me to be all that I could be. He also told me once that my writing was terrible. On this occasion, he compelled me and the library accountant with whom I was writing, to work into the wee hours of the night to improve a report we were preparing. In doing so, he taught me much about writing, and about commitment, and also about "creative" approaches to leadership. As leaders will, he sometimes left me (and others I suspect) annoyed and frustrated and wanting to move—which I eventually did by moving from Alberta to Saskatchewan. Even at this distance, I continued to value his opinions and knowledge and sought his counsel in recommending an American librarian that he highly respected for this book. He suggested Dr. James Neal, whom upon calling, I found to be eager to help a colleague and willing to patiently work through the process to prepare this writing, although James did not know me. This willingness, incidentally, is one of the things about this profession that touches my soul: librarians, almost by definition, represent a profession that is willing to help, eager to serve, and respectful of the human dignity of others.

Dr. Ken Haycock, another leader profiled here, who has a keen sense about the right thing to do and who is also very committed to his work. Ken touched my soul by encouraging me to pursue a doctoral degree, observing that I would make an excellent teacher, and in doing so changed my life. He relit a flame, burning imperceptivity low, which held a decades-old desire to achieve this level of education. I am much indebted to Ken for furthering my education beyond the master's level. It was during my master's in library science degree at the University of Alberta that I first met Dr. Marianne Scott.

Marianne visited the school to promote the Canadian Library Association and to tell us about the National Library of Canada. Dr. Scott impressed me greatly with her British presence and strength of character as she spoke about her career and the path she took to become Canada's National Librarian. Although a mere student, I always felt that Dr. Scott treated me with dignity and respect.

Shortly after library school I attended the Snowbird Leadership Institute described in Chapter Four, where I met Ms. Bridget Lamont. Bridget stood out then, and she does so now, as a librarian committed to her work, and fearless in her approach to it, as well as to life. Bridget challenged the attendees at Snowbird to reach beyond themselves, to risk it all, to overcome their fears and to embrace the moment with conviction. While preparing this book, I had the privilege to work with Bridget while her family was dealing with a very serious illness in one of their children. For my part, I sometimes wonder how my heart keeps beating and my breath endures at the mere thought that anything might threaten my own son. If ever I have to endure what Bridget has, or anything related, I will think of her, of her courage and the way in which she so beautifully continued to give to others through such a trying time.

Another great library leader, but more importantly to me, a great friend, is Mr. Stephen Abram who has seen me through my own trying times. Although he may not know this, his presence has more than once given me an arm to lean on, his candor has helped me to keep my own challenges in perspective, his humor has helped me to laugh at myself, and his approach to raising his children has encouraged me to look more broadly at how I raise my own son.

Ms. Jo Bryant has also touched my soul through comments about her children and what she sometimes sacrificed. I can see how Jo has accomplished all she has, for, while standing in an airport awaiting an arrival, she changed my aspirations in perhaps five short minutes. Our brief conversation seems now like a moment suspended in time during which I was moved at a visceral level that marked each cell of my being with *M* for mother. Our conversation reaffirmed that I am a mother first and foremost. I now schedule my work life around my child's life rather than putting work first and fitting in my child in the spaces that remain. The clock this minute as I write reads 11:33 p.m.; my son is asleep with the sound knowledge that his mom is really present for him, following a very good day of school, friends, sports, and a trip to acquire new boots for dirt bike riding.

While I avow to being a parent first, I also greatly admire and respect those who sacrifice living immediately and always with their children and commute between home and distant work. Mr. Scott Bennett was among the first I knew who did this, although I've seen it done much more in recent years and I recall being somewhat in awe that he gave so selflessly to his work. I was equally taken with his grasp of literature. He served as an example of a librarian who is learned and scholarly and he not only carried that wisdom with him but made it manifest in his daily actions, encounters, and interpretations of the world around him. Another library leader, whom I greatly admire because of her presence, dignity, and determination to live her life her way is Ms. Vivienne Monty. There is an integrity in her approach coming from a solid personal foundation that seems to make her a librarian's librarian.

Clearly, for me, each of the library leaders profiled here has touched my soul in various ways. I am gifted to know each of them, and I hope that each of you will feel gifted as you read this chapter in which they share with us their stories, their values, their lives and their dreams.

## Soulful Stories: Aspects of Leadership

Each one of the forenamed individuals has been recognized as an outstanding leader at various levels within organizations, communities, and nations. It has been a great gift to know some of them personally and others through their reputations for excellence. Embedded in each of them is a deep, passionate and soulful commitment to libraries, to information access and through their work, to the broad fostering of human dignity.

Through correspondence and conversation with these leaders, I delved beyond these initial descriptions and introductions, and asked them about specific areas of library leadership. Their responses, which follow, are illuminating and inspiring. They are relayed to you as they were to me, which uses a self-reporting methodology wherein respondents describe themselves. An approach of this nature is potentially subject to critical analysis as is any methodology of this nature. As articulated by Scott Bennett:

> "Know thyself' is good advice for anyone, not least for library administrators. To know oneself accurately and to tell the truth about oneself is difficult. I have tried to do both of these things in responding to these questions. But surely an important methodological problem for your study is its dependence on self-description. It is likely that I and perhaps others will give you far too rosy, far too self-flattering an account of ourselves if only because we know ourselves imperfectly and fail to judge ourselves dispassionately enough. While I have tried to be scrupulously honest in the account of myself offered in these responses, I know how likely it is that others saw me differently from the way I saw myself.

In self-reporting methodologies, there is always the possibility that others would paint a different picture of any given individual. For example, we would likely get different response from those who reported to any given leader, their bosses, their colleagues, and their families. Such layered investigation was not desired in this writing; we will assume that the leaders profiled did their best to be candid and know themselves as well as any other single individual knows them, if not better.

The profiles employed here and the insights they offer are valuable as simply that, profiles of individuals. I do not suggest that they are representational of the norm, of the professional community, or even of library leaders. They are, in short, either friends or colleagues whom I respect as leaders. The transferability of these ideas to others is spurious, certainly, but that in and of itself does not limit the richness of their contributions to this writing. While we all may from time to time wear rose colored glasses, perhaps what this casts then is an ideal hue to which we can aspire. In reading their responses however, I consider their descriptions to be fair and I invite you to make your own determination.

## How Did They Get Here: On Becoming a Librarian

Almost without fail, few set out to become a librarian; of course, there are exceptions to this claim. First, the rule, then the exceptions. Scott Bennett said it well: "Librarianship was, in fact, a second choice of profession for us. But if we came to our work as an afterthought, we rarely have second thoughts about it. Librarians are fiercely loyal to their calling. However belatedly many of us discover this wonderful profession, few of us can imagine being anything else."

In my own experience, this is true. For my part, I swore that I would never become a librarian. However, since the time that I was sixteen, except for a short shift as a photographer and as a master control switcher at a television studio, I have done little else. Although many of us stumbled into this after doing an undergraduate degree, the roots were planted much earlier than that. I skulked around libraries and bookshops, as did James Neal:

> I was the kid who hung out at the local public library after school and on weekends. I was the kid who would spend hours in bookshops looking to buy volumes on history at the cheapest prices with money earned from my paper route. I was the undergraduate student who browsed the stacks in the college library for days and who would travel into New York City to do weekend research at the New York Public Library. I was the graduate student who lived at his carrel in the bowels of the Butler Library at Columbia. Books, reading, and libraries were always a part of my life, but I never understood that there was actually a profession, called librarianship, that made it all possible.

We might have less challenging situations than the following story from Stephen Abram, but for many of us, our childhoods took us to the library:

> The short answer is that I volunteered in my school library from grade six onwards, and was trapped by the people and books I met there. The longer answer is different. As a very smart, nerdy, very small-for-my-age child, I was bullied repeatedly as a child in the schoolyard, classes and halls of the school. Teachers didn't deal with bullying then and still don't. I discovered that the school library was open at recess, lunch and before and after school. I started to "hide-out" there any time I could—and I began to think of the library as my sanctuary. The librarians supported my thirst for knowledge, which wasn't being met in the classroom, they ignored my poor and underdeveloped social skills and treated me as a person, and they allowed me to help in the library, making me feel useful. This support continued in every library I worked in through high school and university.

For others such as Bridget Lamont, it was a haven from a large family of seven children, and for others it was a haven for an only child as was the case for Ernie Ingles, who spent many childhood hours in the Women's Institute Library in Roblin, Manitoba with his greatly adored grandmother and her friends who had gathered to knit and chat. Later, as a teenager taking correspondence courses, Ernie typically studied in the Calgary Public Library, and after completing a master's degree in history, he opted not to pursue a doctorate and teaching career, but as a friend had done before him, to pursue a library degree. With Ernie, as with many, this choice was an iterative one, culminating after many years in the comfort and wonderful learning environment of the library—always a good place to be when one didn't have anywhere else they needed to be. As well as being a sanctuary, and in some cases a second choice, after being diverted from a career in law, as was Jo Bryant, it has also offered for some a second chance. A good number of librarians gravitate toward this profession after a first career in something else. Scott Bennett, for example, first taught for the English department at University of Illinois at Urbana-Champaign, before becoming a librarian.

Ultimately, irrespective of the paths which brought us to this profession, librarianship offered a solid and fulfilling career choice for women, certainly, and also for men, that paid reasonably well and allowed us to feed our children, ourselves and perhaps our parents.

## What Were They Thinking: Aspirations to Lead

While chatting and corresponding with these leaders, I wondered if those who achieve leadership positions set out to do so. What was their intent? What were they thinking? For the most part, they did not set out to achieve these positions, and doing so was in some cases the result of simply heeding the words of a parent, such as those proffered by the mother of Marianne Scott: *Don't be at the end of any man's buzzer*—aspiring not so much as to be something, as to avoid being something else.

Certainly, for educated, insightful members of this generation such as Marianne Scott and Ken Haycock, there was a clear recognition that in the early 1970s sexism was rampant. Within that environment leadership positions for men were readily available particularly in a profession numerically dominated by women. Women were socialized and educated to be teachers and librarians; men were socialized and educated to be school principals and directors. It was indicative of the adage: if a man wanted to rise to the top quickly in his profession, he should enter a profession dominated by women. Much statistical and other research still indicates that gender disparity is still very evident in librarianship.

One woman, Vivienne Monty, who leads from a middle management position, traces her leadership achievement to her early familial experience in which she was socialized toward leadership:

> I wanted to participate, and although I do not think that it was done consciously, involvement was important to me. I also think that my background is critical to this. My father had always been in charge and an entrepreneur who led rather than followed. I am and always was my father's daughter. Parentage and

environment is important. My parents were both take charge type of people who would not take no for an answer if the answer was important enough to them or their set of principles/ethics. If you wanted to change things, you just had to lead the charge yourself and, most times, do it.

Bridget Lamont also had the experience of an influential father:

> Leadership was drilled into me at home by my father. He was a sales executive who has enormous energy and continues to push, challenge, prod, goad and cheer all of his children and grandchildren. He is so POSITIVE. I was, and still am, reminded I am the "first"—not the oldest (at least that stopped after 40) and that I was expected to lead the way for the others . . . I was always driven and once I reached a goal, was looking for the next. After shelving, I wanted to be in charge of the summer reading program. At the State Library, I thought the pinnacle of my career would be to become a consultant. After a couple of years, I wanted more: Associate Director, Deputy and then Director.

For Jo Bryant, leadership potential was identified by others in her as a teenager:

> I thought that I would work for a few years, get married, and leave the profession. I had always assumed leadership positions, attended a leadership camp and was told by a high school teacher that I had leadership potential. However, I did not see myself as someone who would do this, although I did not necessarily understand what it meant at the time.

For others such as Ernie Ingles, there were those who were not certain they would get a job, let alone one entailing leadership. However, for people such as those who set very high standards for themselves, leadership is almost inevitable. Yet, in Ernie's case he charmingly added that as a young man he thought rather highly of himself, well, at least, more so then than now.

Finally, some set out with the intent to avoid leadership, indicating that the concept of leadership runs counter to their own ideological beliefs, as noted by Scott Bennett: "Beyond this lack of experience with leadership, I was ideologically ill-disposed toward the concept. My interest in socialism led me to believe (not very perceptively) in communal achievement independent of individual leadership." Perhaps achieving leadership positions for individuals such as Scott is somewhat attributable to his ideology of equity, which underpins many theories of successful leadership today.

## What Were They Up To: Assuming Leadership

### *Taking Advantage of Opportunity*

For most of the leaders profiled here, a confluence of circumstance, chance, and opportunity allowed them to assume leadership positions, and success in one endeavor lead to success in others. A strong work ethic, energy and motivation were recognized early in their careers by other people who then gave these leaders confidence which reinforced chances for success. This process enables leaders to achieve greater comfort levels with risk, as well as provides more opportunities to learn about what matters to themselves and to others. Such experiences also groom leaders to see potential in events, comments, feedback, or sets of circumstances that can be leveraged into future achievements.

Bridget Lamont characterizes the coming to leadership as a process. She notes that although we may drive ourselves to excel and accomplish, leadership requires that others call us to lead. In this way, leadership is iterative: if a person does well and accomplishes something, others notice and suggest them for another key role. Colleagues recognize effective and productive leaders and when an organization or community is pursuing a project, they call upon those with a history of success for advice or assistance. Through this process, leaders are identified and created. For Bridget as well, drive, energy, self-confidence, and the ability to make compelling arguments that convince others resulted in her achieving leadership positions. The high school experience of failing to be elected to a leadership position and the subsequent advice of a friend who had been in government for a long time taught her to strategize as well: rather than seeking positions in order to be involved, she chose to seek work in selected areas, such as those that others avoided. Through this insight and strategy, Bridget built a reputation as someone who accomplished things, and was successful in challenging arenas.

## Networking

Jo Bryant had no grand plan to become a leader, and the options of the day were either to get married and be supported by someone else, or to have a profession and support herself. Her appointment as CEO for North York Public Library was her first leadership position, and the decision to apply or not took some consideration. Two retired, male board members encouraged her to do so, which aided her self-confidence, but two female members of the same board discouraged her. Prior to that, she was often fast-tracked and promoted so she obviously had certain skills that were recognized, and she enjoyed being a leader rather than a follower. Ultimately, she decided to apply for the position, and was successful in her bid. Beyond networking to achieve a position, one must develop the skills to perform well and succeed in the position. Becoming a chief librarian required that Jo develop self-awareness; achieving a master's degree in Public Administration gave her an appreciation for the role of libraries within the broader community, which combined to aid her success as a leader.

## What Enables Them to Lead: Qualities of Leadership

Many human qualities have been claimed to be at the heart of leadership, and these have varied over time and have differed according to the person compiling the list. Like leadership itself, leadership qualities are social constructs, and the list for librarianship may differ from the list for other occupations, within other cultures, or throughout other points in our social, cultural, and economic histories. There is no one list that captures leadership, and no leader that has all of the qualities identified on any given list. We can, however, consider some aspects of leadership. The list presented here is what the library leaders profiled in this book consider to be important.

## *Vision*

A leader must be able to envision an alternate reality in which they truly believe. Part of this, according to Jo Bryant, is to see that big picture, and also to recognize where the library fits into the bigger picture. For Jo, part of that bigger picture is revealed through her deep interest in the city of Toronto. She loves urban life: the feels, the smells, the noise, the excitement, and the challenge that urban issues present. She understands the role played by the public in the whole mix, and that the library is deeply appreciated for what it offers. She is concerned about what happens in a downtown urban area when it allows its institutions to deteriorate, and works hard to counter that. To achieve this or any vision requires the ability to attract a strong team of performers committed to the vision; successful people and strong leaders have good people around them. Leaders who want to be singly and solely the star performer attract less capable people in order to ensure that there is limited competition. But this ultimately limits the chances of a leader's success.

To achieve vision, Stephen Abram tries to live in the future. He actively monitors futurists' e-lists and publications, and has founded a few futurists groups. He reads books and articles about predictions, trends, and forecasting; writes and speaks about the future in order to form and clarify his thoughts; and makes services and products that will work better in the future than they do in the present. He monitors generational change and changes in behaviors across generational cohorts to see what future they are prepared for, tracks popular culture and fads, and watches toys to discover innovations in play which may point to trends.

Vivienne Monty dreams of desired states, as had her patents before her. Her parents knew that many of their dreams would never be realized but that didn't stop them from striving. Vivienne saw them achieve many of the things they dreamed of, and recognized the effort to be worthwhile. She typically tries to think outside of the box. For her, the heart of leadership is dreams premised upon insight and translated through influence. It involves a process of knowing that something needs to be done, understanding what should be done, and accomplishing one's objectives. Leading from the middle, she believes that consensus-building and collaborative effort are the best ways in which to do that. Her approach incorporates setting examples of growth, progress, and influence. This is hard work, but it is the best way to encourage others to follow one's lead through sound communication, networking, and altruistic goals aimed at a common good that meets the needs of all involved.

Ken Haycock noted that if one has self-confidence and a wide circle of friends and acquaintances, together with a passion for one's profession, it is difficult to avoid having vision. One can then see patterns, connections, possibilities, and how people's lives can be changed. Ken insightfully noted that because our profession is so misunderstood, it is easier to provide fresh insights, value-added propositions, and overlay business and community development perspectives, precisely because few have thought about the library's contribution in these areas. Or, if they have thought much about libraries, it is only in limited and constrained ways. Advocates may well promote "library, library, library," but we also need to be players at the table, demonstrating value and impact for our clients, be that within the realms of student achievement, economic development, research productivity, or quality of life.

For others, such as Marianne Scott, one may not see a defined vision, per se, but a need, and is motivated by that recognized need. Such an approach serves one well in terms of transforming the need into an objective or set of goals and then delineating strategies to meet the desired ends.

Similarly, Scott Bennett claimed to have little vision of (or for) librarianship. What he does have is a set of personal values shaped by a commitment to teaching and learning, intelligence and a quick understanding, the wish to listen to others and to learn from them, good professional sense, and an often astute feeling for the environment of academic libraries and tactics for getting things done. None of these qualities generate a vision of what librarianship or libraries should be, but all of these qualities contributed to the success of the libraries in which he worked. The skills he valued most highly, in himself and others, were tactical (but not necessarily timorous or unimaginative) ones—the ability to read the environment shrewdly and discover the right and true thing to do. A practical consequence of being visionless is that Scott embraced strategic action but disavowed strategic planning.

Taking these ideas together, Ernie Ingles has mastered both a compelling vision and recognition of the role that others play in vision creation. He suspects that he is among the world's greatest vagabonds and thieves in his ability to understand, internalize, and use the insights and the ideas of others. Ernie has the unique capacity to listen—really listen—to what others are saying, and understand things in a way that they themselves perhaps do not. He sees the potential, the implications and the underlying imperatives of the ideas, insights, and suppositions of those with whom he works and interacts. Once he internalizes an idea, he has the initial courage to operationalize the vision, the motivating passion to undertake action, and the sustaining tenacity to realize his goals. This latter aspect of leadership, that of tenacity, is a critical element that indicates sustainable leadership. In my view, it is one thing to launch a project and yet quite another to see it through under all odds and when subjected to much adversity. I have been blessed to witness in Ernie what aboriginal cultures characterize as bison in a snowstorm. Elders tell of the bison, which when walking into an oncoming blinding storm, have the opportunity to make a decision. They might either turn around and go back in the direction they came, or they may proceed and seek calmer and clearer skies ahead. Wanting to reach their destination, and knowing that that they walked into a storm and that in turning around it may simply follow them, they soldier forward, through the storm to reach their desired end. Sometimes too as we each struggle through our personal and professional storms, it may help to remind ourselves to continue to put one foot in front of the other, one step at a time. Ernie learned this as a very young boy when he contracted polio, not once but twice, and could merely hobble around on crutches for the first decade of his life. When he finally could walk, he then took up tap dancing (for those of you who know him: *can you imagine?*) Today, to achieve his vision, he marches onward with the determination of a tenacious soldier and pussyfoots with the sophistication of an alley cat (or a tap dancer) negotiating a minefield.

### *Passion and Advocacy*

Passion is central to leadership. Without it, it is difficult to create visions, to dream, to do, and to inspire. Peter Bender who wrote *Leadership from Within* (1997) asserts that while vision leads us forward, passion drives us forward. What inspires passion for the leaders I encountered focused on ideals or values as well as on people—colleagues, library users, family, and humanity. Ernie Ingles believes that libraries, be they academic, public or special, are inherently good things and important places and that they make a difference in people's lives. Inspiring children to read, students to learn, or adults to broaden their worlds, and easing the access to the materials they need in order to do so is crucial. For him, passion comes from a fundamental belief system and a set of values premised upon the enhancement of humanity. While that may sound grandiose, it can be seen in the youngest child who simply wants to borrow a book, to the most elderly seeking solace in the twilight. In this regard, Ernie believes that our work is underrated, and that our profession has had an enormous impact on the lives of many, and on society generally.

Marianne Scott is inspired in her work through engagement with colleagues and friends. They sustain her belief in librarianship and in the Canadian Library Association, and motivated her "fighting blood" as she described her tendency to speak out when she felt it was necessary to do so.

Similarly, Stephen Abram, a man very focused on family, finds that his children and their friends inspire passion for him. Stephan wants young people to have a world in which libraries are about more than information; they are about knowledge, innovation, culture, learning, and life. In this, passion for work is integrated into passion for life—a desire to do the right things for the right reasons—which is what many call advocacy.

Jo Bryant also finds integration between libraries and life as central to her work as a public librarian. She is inspired by seeing the impact that the public library has on the quality of life in Toronto and in the lives of its people, especially children. Programs focused on children at Toronto Public Library have been premised upon the desire to improve the lives of children, particularly those who don't have the support they need. Jo has seen what a difference her staff has made, and believes very deeply that the public library contributes greatly to the quality of life in her community.

Ken Haycock lights upon the idea that passion for the profession comes from within the profession itself and the close connection this has to his entire life including personal elements:

> My profession and work is a passion for me. If I didn't enjoy my work immensely I would do something else. It's as simple as that. If you love your work and you believe that you can make a positive difference, why wouldn't you put time and energy into your pursuits? Some people enjoy television; some enjoy sports; some enjoy their children and grandchildren—I enjoy my primary relationship (enhanced by friends, travel, culture, dining, etc.) and my work (similarly enhanced by community and association involvement).

While some might argue that what one does is separate from who one is, it is not always so simple to draw such clear distinctions. For some people in some professions, what one does and who one is can be interconnected. This seems to be the case for many library leaders who are passionate about their work.

What about your own passion? Peter Urs Bender (1997) believes that as children we all start out with passion. We love to explore, create and learn new things. We have a vision of what we can do and who we can become, and for a variety of reasons we tend to lose this over time. Our personal passion does need to be replenished periodically and can be nurtured and reclaimed. To find your passion, be aware of your feelings and your vision;

identify those things to which you give yourself wholeheartedly; and, pay attention to instances in which you use words like *love, enjoy, easy, care about*, and *great*. And if you are still struggling to find your passion, remember to lighten up, laugh lots and hang out with those who have passion—maybe through theirs you will discover your own. In the final accounting, it is passion that makes the difference. The Greeks, for example, did not write obituaries upon death; they asked only one question: *Did he have passion?*

### *Courage and Initiative*

Oscar Wilde observed, "There was no pleasure I did not experience. I threw the pearl of my soul into a cup of wine. I went down the primrose path to the sound of flutes. I lived on honeycomb. But to have continued the same life would have been wrong because it would have been limiting. I had to pass on. The other half of the garden had its secrets for me also" (Wilde, 1911, p. 65). Along with passion, courage and initiative are essential in life and in leadership.

Ernie Ingles believes that the willingness to recognize opportunity and then to take the risk to pursue those opportunities is an important element of leadership. He notes, however, that some opportunities should not be pursued and some risks should not be taken. The question in my mind remains: How does one know which opportunities to pursue and which are to be avoided?

Embedded in this question is ambiguity, which Stephen Abram observes is at the heart of leadership. Change involves a multitude of factors, some indicating that the vision is simply faulty or clearly inappropriate, or that the process of change is flawed. Unless one can deal with ambiguity throughout the process from project selection to completion, one will likely fail. Major skills in dealing with ambiguity include having a tenacious focus on the power of the visionary goal and modeling to others a behavior and belief in its successful attainment.

Vivienne Monty asserts that taking initiative in the first instance is critical. One can be a sheep or the shepherd. She says: "It never ceases to amaze me that when I take initiative for something, others suddenly say, 'Oh golly, I had just meant to do that or I was just thinking of doing that.' Why they never do IT is beyond me—they simply wait for the other guy." In leading from the middle, she believes that one should seek to make the changes they would like to see in projects where they have influence. In doing so, some situations may require selectively questioning the choices or decisions of higher authority or being prepared to take calculated risks that others would avoid.

## *Communication*

For Stephen Abram and Ernie Ingles, the ability to articulate a clear expression of ideas and goals is a primary skill for leaders. Clear communication, in many forms including written and spoken, as well as the ability to listen to individuals and groups, are all necessary for good leadership. In order to articulate a vision, inspire passion and motivate others to action, as well to explain why an opportunity is a good one, or conversely, why it is not, one must have excellent communication skills. Moreover, in daily leadership tasks, it is well also to remember that in the absence of information, people make up their own. Communicating well avoids the creation and dissemination of wrong information.

## *Stewardship, Truthfulness, and Joy*

In the view of Scott Bennett, the three most critical elements of leadership are stewardship, truthfulness, and joy:

> *Stewardship:* Leadership is fundamentally an exercise of self-denying responsibility to others. In his book titled *Stewardship* (1993), Peter Block defines the activity as "choosing service over self-interest." The ideas of Block that have particular power for me are those of choosing partnership, of choosing adventure over safety, and of hope triumphing over experience. I once defined myself as a steward of the Yale University Library to a distinguished and very generous supporter of that library, who spent his professional lifetime in Boston being the steward of other people's wealth. He doubted I meant what I said and thought I should describe my work in grander terms. The comic paradox, of course, is that the choice of stewardship can be immensely self-gratifying, materially rewarding, and lead to

considerable professional prominence. In my case, I held one of the most highly regarded positions in academic libraries in North America, was often asked to do things because of that position, and was very well paid to boot. *Truthfulness:* Personal integrity is an aspect of truthfulness that is often listed as a key leadership attribute. It is surely that, but I suppose integrity must be grounded in a conviction that truth exists, an idea that is not congenial to our relativistic age. One can domesticate this radical view about truth through a commitment to evidence, multiplicity of views, dispassionate reasoning and discourse, and—hardest of all—a fearless resolve to act on one's best (if imperfect) perception of what is true. This resolve is what drives the choice of adventure over safety. While I am sure truth exists, I also know that it is extremely difficult to know. (The commonplace contrast between God's infinite and our finite knowledge express this idea.) There is nothing to do about this fact except to acknowledge it by viewing one's professional life as fundamentally a teaching and learning endeavor. *Joyful teaching and learning:* I affirm that teaching and learning should be joyful. I think leaders must visibly show joy in their work and must find ways to help create a joyful (which is different from an enjoyable) environment for work. Such an environment affirms the work of the library and the people who do it; it affirms the readers who are served; and it affirms the larger enterprise of which the library is a part (the creation, transmission, and preservation of knowledge in the case of an academic library). Most fundamentally, leadership should affirm the comic possibilities of life (the triumph of hope over experience, to use Block's words). It is the revelation of these comic possibilities that most infuses teaching and learning with joy.

Where among these three elements does the heart of leadership lie? It lies in all of them, when taken together. The three are inextricable parts, one of the other. The choice for something other than self-interest is a choice for truth, and this choice can only be made (given our most imperfect ability to know what is true) through a deep commitment to teaching and learning. That commitment is best sustained by the joy of its often comic outcomes.

## *Focus and Innovation*

For Stephen Abram, focus and innovation are two main elements of leadership:

> If you don't focus yourself and your team on the few key issues that will make a difference, then you diffuse your energy and efforts too widely and achieve too little. You also need to focus on process over almost everything else. If the process isn't right then you can easily go off track. If you're not innovating, then what are you leading toward, the status quo? Keeping things at status quo—stable and operational—is just management, not leadership. Leadership is about change. Therefore you must innovate and invent or be able to recognize and lead appropriate innovation in order to be a leader.

## *Subject Knowledge and Skill*

It has been argued that once you know how to manage, you can manage anything. Vivienne Monty believes this is simply not so. She asserts that one must have a sound foundation within the discipline:

> Managing a glove factory and a library might have some principles in common but it's not the same thing and different sets of skills are required. I will never forget about 20 some years ago my staff telling me that they loved coming with me to professional meetings because I knew the subject matter so well and always knew what types of questions to ask. They told me that my subject knowledge made them proud and feel that I would follow the right paths. As a reference librarian many have told me they come to me because I understand what it is they want in their subject area. This might be considered gaining leadership authority and respect through subject knowledge.

## *Giving Credit*

Marianne Scott found throughout her career that to appreciate the work of others, to give credit to those who do the work, to thank them, reward them, and recognize them, goes a long way toward leading well and to continuing to inspire dedication and nurture continued motivation.

# What Keeps Them Going: Motivational and Sustaining Elements of Leadership

## *Motivation*

I asked the leaders with whom I spoke what motivated them to put leadership energy into their work. Motivation, for Scott Bennett, was instilled through the commitment of a parent:

> My father was a self-made man in the conventional meaning of that phrase, and I do not doubt that I unwittingly learned from him a commitment to work. Beyond that, it has always been inconceivable to me to work at something that was not important, and not to work with all of one's energy at something that is important. Since sometime in high school, I have never been able to engage in my studies or my work with anything but full-hearted energy. I learned from reading John Ruskin to value, not the perfect execution of one's work, but the spiritual aspect of any work done earnestly.

For others, motivation is derived from a strong belief in what they are doing or the contribution they see they could make. Marianne Scott observed: "Leadership energy comes from believing in library ideals; librarians are essentially socially minded and activist oriented, who recognize that it is our job to make information available to those who do not have it." Stephen Abram also aspires to high ideals, and in that aspiration he recognized that he could influence social outcome: "I want to have a positive future. I want to leave a footprint on the world that says I was here and made a positive difference. Otherwise I'll just have breathed air and eaten food and taken up space that some more valuable person could have had."

Ernie Ingles agrees that while one must believe in what they are doing, people can be highly motivated by their ego which compels them to do the work to achieve the difference they envision. Jo Bryant notes, candidly, that negative emotion sometimes motivates her; she recalled at times being driven by a fear of failure. As described earlier, she has a powerful need to succeed, both for herself, her organization, and her community.

## *Values and Occasional Compromise*

> *Always act in accordance with the dictates of your conscience,*
> *my boy, and chance the consequences.*

—Pirate King to Frederic, Act I of Gilbert and Sullivan's
*The Pirates of Penzance*

Acting on the dictates of your conscience was the goal to which Pirate King aspired; similarly, leaders have, and attend to, ethical principles. These principles are derived from values and beliefs about what is correct, fair, and just—judgments that are learned and internalized through social conditioning based on social mores. Sometimes, due either to administrative ambiguity or political pressure, ethical principles are occasionally compromised, which may be done in order to balance or accommodate conflicting ethical principles. An example of such conflict was offered by Ken Haycock:

> I had a senior position where I was privy to budget information and knowledgeable of the implications of budget reduction exercises on individuals and important units of the organization and was unable to advise people of decisions they should be taking to land on their feet. There are, of course, inalienable ethical principles, but there is also a hierarchy of "goods" and confidentiality for the good of the overall organization, and hundreds of employees, which took precedence over helping the few who were known to me. Obviously, in the end, my colleagues felt somewhat betrayed by me on an emotional level while recognizing my lack of options, short of resigning, which would have made no difference to the final decisions. No one ever accused me of not advocating vigorously and effectively for their programs and positions; no one ever questioned my integrity or ethics; it was, nevertheless, difficult and stressful.

Another example has to do with maintaining pay equity among the professional librarians at Yale (the support staff are paid under a negotiated labor contract). Given salary administration practices, the ultimate responsibility for implementing the "equal pay for equal work" principle fell to

Scott Bennett as University Librarian. In the last couple of years, it became increasingly difficult to maintain this principle as they hired excellent people with highly specialized subject matter or language skills. They frequently found that market pressures in making these new hires required some inventive arguments regarding the comparable qualifications and duties of existing staff. Sometimes no amount of ingenuity could save them from the bald fact that the new hire's salary was out of line with that of others. He took some comfort from a book by Peter Cappelli arguing that the "new economy" required employers and employees alike to abandon "old fashioned" notions of equity within the organization and to embrace the larger market for human skills as the only arbiter of equity. There was little comfort in this argument, however. He understood the rationality of Cappelli's argument, but it had little real power against a professional lifetime of concern (especially in a profession where women are a majority) about pay equity.

The second example involved a Black History Month exhibit at the Milton S. Eisenhower Library at Johns Hopkins University, where Scott Bennett was the Library Director. One year the library exhibited material from their abolitionist collection. A group of black students visited Scott to protest the exhibit, claiming it insensitively showed blacks as the objects of other persons' action rather than as shaping their own history. Of this, Scott writes:

> The students wanted the exhibit removed and a new one installed. I agreed our exhibit had the character the students described and could be understood as insensitive. I affirmed that I and my colleagues had learned from what the students said and that future exhibits would not be offensive in this way. I said it would be impractical to mount a new exhibit with half of the celebratory month behind us. I thought (incorrectly) that the promise to avoid the mistake of the current exhibit in future exhibits was responsive to the students' concerns. That is, I thought our purpose was a mutual engagement with teaching and learning, and the exhibit had been a most useful instrument for this.

The students said nothing more to me until, on the second last day of February, they occupied the library late in the evening and prevented it from being closed. They demanded that the abolitionist literature exhibit be immediately taken down and a new one installed. They would not leave the building until these demands were met. I arrived at the library, in response to a police call, sometime shortly after midnight. I said the exhibit was the work of others in the library, as would be a new exhibit, and that I could not dismount the exhibit or agree to a new one without first consulting those colleagues. I was trying to teach the protesting students something about the conduct of academic life and discourse. They were not interested and had purposes other than such learning; they insisted on dismounting the exhibit. They threatened to break into the exhibit cases and remove the materials themselves if I did not. My choices were to ask the police to arrest the protesters and clear the building, to endanger the safety of people and library collections by letting the students act on their threat, or to take the exhibit down myself. I did the latter, which I do not doubt was an expedient, prudent thing to do. The threat of violence constituted, however, an utter abnegation of the reasoned discourse that defines higher education and to which I am deeply committed. The assertion of power prevailed over any possibility for learning from one other about anything other than the assertion of power itself. I said this to the students at the time. They were quite unmoved by what I would describe as an educator's argument; they knew they had me in their power, and that is what they wanted.

So I learned about power, and the lesson was reinforced as I saw the Provost's office—itself the target of other activities by the black students—distance itself from my problems. I learned too about the generosity of the Eisenhower Library staff, as they set about in less than a week's time to create a new Black history exhibit and as they comforted me personally. I needed this, not least of which was because the day following the midnight demonstration was also stressful. There were the ordinary crisis management activities that filled the day until late afternoon, when there was a public meeting demanded by students to force an apology from me for the abolitionist exhibit. I was little inclined to apologize (having not yet learned that the issue was the exercise of student power and not, as I thought it should be, due regard for the professional judgment of my library colleagues or the educational opportunities of the disagreement

I don't think anyone could say no to [the question of ethical compromise]. In fact, my story is one where my personal ethics and professional ethics collided. It was a reference question that I found personally offensive (a client, Japanese manufacturer, wanted me to find lists of Japanese in Canada to hire for managing their new plant because they would work harder than Canadians), colliding with my professional responsibility to give good service and to meet the user's needs. I managed this by properly providing sources to advertise the positions in and also provided the advertising, labor codes, and legal and liability issues that they could encounter if they chose to try this tactic.

If one is really lucky, perhaps these situations can be avoided ogether. Vivienne Monty felt that very rarely has she been ked to compromise her principles or ethics and when it has curred, she refused, believing that living with oneself is ramount.

In other situations, compromise is a matter of opinion. idget Lamont indicated that while some might say that she did mpromise, she did not agree:

In one afternoon, the library budget for one line item was cut 33 percent. Libraries had never been cut before; the agencies in this line item were used to getting what they wanted with minimal interference from the state library. The call came to me and I had to make a fast decision—fight it or accept it and deal with it. I accepted it, and was asked to call the affected agencies myself. I then lived through a bomb threat, a death threat, horrid press, and personal attacks for six months. It was a good decision in three ways: 1) I proved my loyalty to the person who had hired me; 2) that loyalty yielded the development of a massive new funding source for libraries later that year; 3) some of the agencies were jolted out of complacency and the concept of "new paradigms" was put to an immediate test. The anger and damage never left for some people but we all survived and learned.

Similarly, when it comes to political forums and compromise, arianne Scott replied: "We all have compromised, even though u may not believe in doing it." In political arenas, it was

about the exhibit), and I initially refused to do so. Th
students said they would reoccupy the library and sta
I apologized. I recognized I had no choice at this
apologized. The students' response to this forced an
action was publicly to declare that a person who wou
to his principles should not be entrusted with a 
position in an institution of learning. I had been v
adrenaline for something like thirty hours and found t
utterly demoralizing.

I add two things to this story. The first is that in
evening, after the personally devastating public n
couple of students came to the office to ask to see
explained they were among the protesting students,
wanted me to know the attack on me was not meant p
This flabbergasted me, though I quite believed this sta
their intention. Sometime later I concluded these stud
much to learn about the heedless "collateral damage" th
can cause in pursuing a principled political goa
mindedly. The second addendum concerns a visit to t
Hopkins campus by Archbishop Tutu about a year l
Archbishop spoke movingly of the faith in the goo
people that had sustained him through decades of oppo
apartheid in South Africa. At the end of the assembl
black students rose and asked the Archbishop to join 
opposing what they saw as the racist behaviors of the un
Archbishop Tutu was simply beautiful. He gently dec
champion the students' cause, reminding them that his t
been about charity and good faith and not political pow
is the only comedy I have ever been able to find in what 
me an extremely painful encounter with political activisn
the assembly hoping against hope the black student
willing to learn something from Archbishop Tutu.

Sometimes, it seems that our ethical principles b
those of others, or so it would seem. In these cases, we 
no choice but to "compromise" ours in order to valida
which may involve determining whose issue it is to d
whose principles should take precedence. No small matt
sure. Sometimes, if we are lucky and clever enough, we 
a way to accommodate without compromise, such as 
Abram did in the following story:

sometimes necessary to "bite one's tongue" particularly when the consequences of speaking out are very strong. One needs to be politically astute and remember the end game, she noted, which in her case was to promote the interests of the National Library of Canada.

### *Instincts*

Considering the role instincts play in leadership is not an easy question. Instincts are difficult to define. I read on a poster once: *make the small decisions with your head, and the big decisions with your heart.* (As if it were that simple.) Perhaps instincts are related to what is felt in your heart, or in the pit of your stomach, or in the recesses of your brain.

However instincts are defined or characterized, Ken Haycock believes that they are critical to success. They allow you to pose questions, and assess responses on a number of levels, incorporating best guesses when base data is not available. For example, one might ask such questions as: Is this the ditch I want to die in? What is the worst thing that could happen as a result of this decision? Is this person trustworthy? Why am I uncomfortable with what I am being told here? In evaluating potential responses to questions, calling upon experience improves instincts.

Instincts are used in various ways. For example, Vivienne Monty uses them for a sense of timing and relies on them to advise her about when to move on, when to act, and when to use caution. Marianne Scott depends a lot on instincts, particularly in hiring, and would sometimes look at references only after she had decided to hire.

Bridget Lamont believes that instincts have contributed greatly to what she has accomplished. She doesn't deliberate for long periods and doesn't overanalyze. She is inclined to seize opportunities rather than to plan for months, and uses instincts to create new alliances, find advocates, and open doors.

Stephen Abram uses his instincts for three purposes. First, it tells him where to look for new changes. His instincts make suggestions about new ideas and change, and provide clues about where to start looking for evidence. Second, they tell him if something is offending his value system. He says, "If I get tense or knotted up, I try to remember to think if I'm doing something that's going to bother me in my sleep. I ask myself the question: What keeps me awake at night? The answer to that tells me where my instincts are going. Of course, then I have to look for evidence." Thirdly, he uses instinct for major decisions. He claims that you can never have enough data to support a difficult decision—at some point you have to take a risk and use instincts to decide what is the best course of action. He observes that some people overanalyze and would be well served by trusting informed instincts in order to lead in a timely way.

Scott Bennett feels he did less well when he employed his instincts in decision making; a quick intelligence left him feeling he saw issues more clearly than others and impatient to express that clarity of understanding and to act on it. He more often succeeded when he committed himself to consciously attempting to listen to and learn from others.

Ernie Ingles has always relied on instincts. He uses them in decision-making processes and public speaking. He feels that he can read an audience through a sensory envelope that is very keen and aware of those around him. He has a sense of what people are thinking and what they need in order to be motivated.

Instincts are used to greater and lesser degrees by leaders, for different purposes. Such use is well complemented by informed thought, careful deliberation, and communication with others.

## *Satisfaction and Spirituality*

A prevalent theme among library leaders concerning satisfaction in library work was working closely with others in a spirit of partnership and collegiality with a shared desire to create something of excellence that has great value for individuals or a collective. Scott Bennett notes: "My colleagues and I regularly recognized that our ability to achieve excellence and perform well was absolutely dependent on our effectiveness in working together."

Satisfaction comes through seeing library users and staff excited about libraries and the richness they bring to lives of individuals as well as equity to communities. A number of library leaders noted great enjoyment in watching the look in the eyes of children and adults when things come together well in the library; they enjoy the smiling faces, the wonderment, the awe, and sometimes the tears. They feel they have done a fine day's work when they have done something to make someone else's day, or when they have helped others accomplish their goals.

Jo Bryant puts this into context with her administrative responsibilities: Of necessity she administers a bureaucratic process which is not terrible exciting. However, a motivational factor for her is the opportunity to create a truly magnificent public library; she knows what the library system can do and works toward that end. Ultimately, seeing the library filled with people is often the highlight of her day.

Ernie Ingles gets satisfaction from watching the successes of others, and watching what grows from the seeds that he has planted. He believes that he has certainly experienced a spiritual dimension in his work. One easily identified arena in which this occurs is at Northern Exposure to Leadership, which itself has spiritual components. Yet, he adds, there are also spiritual dimensions in one's vision, passion, and desire to make a difference that is premised upon one's values.

A number of leaders identified a spiritual dimension to their work which brings satisfaction, and that this concept is closely related to passion and caring deeply about libraries, the services they provide, and the significant impact they have on peoples' lives. Marianne Scott characterized some aspects of her work as spiritual which draw upon moral codes of fairness in decision making, decision making that is based on idealism and democracy. Jo Bryant concurred and added that treating people well, and being honest and straightforward involved a spirituality rooted in her Catholic upbringing. This resonated for me as a Catholic, but I can also relate very strongly to Stephen Abram who indicated that although he is not particularly religious, he does enjoy using prediction methodologies found in many spiritual quests: Delphi methods, I Ching, Dice, Ouiji, and an encyclopedia of divination methods. He uses these to break up staid organizational thinking and to incite innovation. He also finds respite from the technocracy of work by reading Haiku, poetry, Tao, Bhuddist and other eastern philosophies, books of quotes, and so on.

Like Russ Moxley who wrote *Leadership and Spirit: Breathing New Vitality and Energy into Individuals and Organizations* (2000), when I use the word spirit, I am not referring to religion or the tenets of any particular religion, or even concerned about achieving an elevated state of mind or being through prayer or meditation. Like Moxley, being spiritual is being fully human, integrating all energies that are a part of us, and connecting to a life force that is part of us and connects us. Moxley asserts that spirit in the workplace breathes vitality and energy into individuals and organizations. He defines spirit from the Latin *spiritus*, which means breath and breathe. Moxley recognizes that four elements of an individual go to work each day, the physical (we sit, walk, travel), the mental (we think, assess, strategize), the emotional (we feel happy, sad, elated, crestfallen), and the spiritual (the most likely to be overlooked), and all must be recognized and integrated in the workplace. Spirit allows us to offer our whole selves in the work place, to make deep connections with others, and to find meaning and richness in our work that is motivational and inspirational. This is particularly important when the modern workplace requires creativity and passion of its leaders.

Stephen Abram ponders:

> Is the essence of the soul (or spirit) of librarianship discovered when we find it being soulless? For instance, when we talk about virtual libraries—where sometimes the human element is excised and/or devalued—are we not most offended by the soullessness of the 'product'? Do we find our professional souls in the service aspects and human aspects of our jobs? When we see reference work done perfunctorily without a care for the ends of the user or added value in terms of analysis or interpretation—is that not soulless? Our work is degraded—and so is our profession—when we accept 'minimum' standards of transactional delivery instead of looking at every user interaction as a transformational act—a moment of truth and learning.

While we seek to find the laudable values of satisfaction and a sense of spiritual fulfillment in our work, either through its existence or its absence, we are served well to remember that true satisfaction and spiritual fulfillment in life requires balance.

### *Balancing Competing Demands*

In the case of most of the leaders profiled, either they or their families felt that balance between work and life was not successfully achieved. Scott Bennett did not think he was a workaholic, but his wife maintained that he always behaved like one. That's telling. There certainly was never a time, in either his student or professional life, when he did not work very long hours. As sometimes happens, one member of a couple seeks to move along in their career and that necessitates moving along in their home. In the case of Scott and his wife, the latter of whom did not want to move, they agreed that they would each live where they preferred, which resulted in them living in different cities for twenty years and commuting. This arrangement assumed different forms as the years passed, and they remained a loving couple and their children have become healthy, responsible adults. By these measures, Scott feels that they managed the competing demands of work and home fairly successfully.

For James Neal, keeping work and home in balance is a constant challenge. His spouse worked for decades as an accountant with complete job and geographic flexibility and with a willingness to relocate every six or seven years which made his administrative advancement possible. James' wife also gave him the space to work evenings and to travel often to conferences and meetings, which allowed his professional career to advance. Although he was very committed to his work, James was still actively involved in his daughter's life as well as engaged with a rich network of friends.

Stephen Abram claims not to balance home and work very well, but makes definite attempts to do so. At one point, he changed jobs to get more evening and weekend time. He believes that quantity time is better with family, compared to quality time, which evolves into a rationalization for too little time. He meets the objective of spending more time with his children by integrating his interests with those of his children, who enjoy attending movies and live theatre, visiting art galleries and museums, eating dinner out and watching TV. He also takes a film course every winter with his son. With direct attention paid to family time, it makes it more attainable to give his family top priority and leave work no matter what when there is a conflict. What Stephen feels is sometimes lost in the shuffle is time for himself, and with his very high performing children who themselves are busy, it is also challenging to have his children make time for him.

A number of female library leaders have forgone having children and the question of balance becomes somewhat less complicated, although they too can tend to overextend themselves at work. In most cases, priority was given to work early in one's career and private lives assume more importance once careers are established. Of a particular generation too, the depression years forced a concentration on career, particularly for Marianne Scott who cared for her mother without support of extended family. There was no guilt in leaving children or a husband while she worked because as she didn't have these. There may have been some guilt in leaving her mother alone while she worked, but any potential for that was offset by the support and encouragement for her work that Marianne received from her mother. Marianne at times missed quality personal time for herself and with her mother, but work provided her with a social life, and so some measure of balance was achieved in her social life. That, however, was premised upon colleagues and work-related activities.

Jo Bryant was a library leader with children who found balance between work and home to be a challenge. She raised two boys while working full-time. Jo was divorced and remarried, but always had the support of her partners. With that support, she was able to move easily from the workplace to home, and typically was able to leave the office at the end of the day. This was also enabled by the support systems that are available for parents such as good day cares, reasonable employers, and people in the background who helped. She acknowledges that her children might have a different perspective, however, and recalls hearing: *Are you going to another meeting, Mom?* At times, things would become too stressful. She has herself suffered from stress from time to time, and is sure that stress periodically affected her mood and her ability to deal patiently with things, as well as to be as careful and comforting a mother as she may have wanted to be. She has some deep regrets about not having had the additional time to devote to children when they were younger and not following the progress of their schooling as acutely as she could have.

Similarly, Bridget Lamont has children and offers some things that she has learned. She acknowledges that when you work and have children, things are rarely done as well as you know you can do them, and consequently a little time gets shaved off for the children and a little time gets shaved off from work. It's too easy to take work home; when you take it home your mind is never fully cleared to concentrate on children, home and family, and so it is wise to try to use the weekends as weekends. Like many, she too wanted it all with her first child, but then she saw how fast time went, and made a decision and an adjustment about a year after being named state librarian. Because she was on the payroll for the state of Illinois, and felt her first obligation was there, she did not attend national and international conferences as her colleagues did and as she would have liked. While she may have envied her colleagues who flew to international IFLA locations, she consoled herself that her time would come. It hasn't in the ways she expected but she remains ever hopeful in the adage "things even out." She reminds us that every year does go faster, and now with a very ill child she knows more than ever before the importance of family, that the only thing that really counts is one's children and what one can do as a parent to help them grow.

Ernie Ingles believes that balance is situational and contextual, and that he has achieved balance in his life. In his case, it was a family approach to careers where both partners dedicated much to their work, and achieved an internal equilibrium that served the family. A significant measure for him to evaluate if balance was achieved is that his daughter,

Erin, is a well-adjusted and happy young woman who benefited from having a father who is a leader. As a young teenager, Ernie took Erin to England, where she later had the unique experience of working for Miles and Briony Blackwell. While parents as leaders give much to their work, there is also some advantage and inherent opportunities that this affords their children.

## *Energy Renewal*

The question of energy renewal is as perpetual as the need for it, and hopefully as perpetual as the answer. Scott Bennett phrases it well:

> It is literally the case that over the last ten years before I retired (in 2001), I quite often found myself asking, as I walked into work in the morning, why I was doing this. I was regularly feeling the deep fatigue of seventy-hour workweeks and dissatisfaction with a personal life lived several hundred miles from my wife. If that was regularly the question of the morning, I just as regularly found its answer during the course of the day. The answer was the chance to work in close partnership with wonderful colleagues to create something of excellence.

He noted further that in his view, and others concurred, that few university faculty or city administrators have much notion of how demanding library administration is. Ultimately, the answers of the evening were not as powerful as the question of the morning, and he retired after a long and fruitful career.

For some, such as James Neal and Stephen Abram, work gives them energy. James works within an academic library which he characterizes as existing within a political campus environment, a political professional environment, and a political information policy environment. James is challenged and energized by the complexities of the politics. He gains his greatest satisfaction from a sense of growth, advancement, accomplishment, relevance, collegial involvement, as well as being a citizen of the university and a contributor to broader professional conversations nationally and globally. His involvement requires regular renewal of energy, which he finds in cultural activities such as plays, concerts, movies as well as in travel, and in his grandchildren. Similarly, Stephen finds energy in being with people. He goes to conferences to rejuvenate, and seeks to spend time with new librarians as much as possible and at least once per month.

For others, such as Jo Bryant, solitude and downtime at the end of the day are required for energy renewal. Jo reserves time for herself, particularly now that her children are grown and away at school. She believes that a life well led leaves time for companionship and conversations with family. Similarly, Marianne Scott is renewed when she leaves work at the office and doesn't take it home with her; this is more successfully done in terms of leaving issues out of her annual vacation carpetbags than leaving them out of her weekly grocery bags.

Energy can be renewed in many ways, and some seek to renew it in ways we would all enjoy, were we so lucky. Although he has a high energy level, Ken finds renewal by going twice yearly on a beach vacation with his wife for a week where they "do nothing (yes, nothing) but vegetate on the beach for seven hours a day and wonder about where we'll go for dinner." He comes back wonderfully renewed and refreshed. To supplement the biannual vacation, he also swims and works out a few times a week, which for him does not necessarily renew energy, but rather is a chore that simply enables him to indulge his interest in eating and drinking without showing it too much.

Ernie Ingles believes that early in his career he had a huge stock of energy, which has waxed and waned from time to time. On the rare occasions when energy waned, Ernie created new incentives and opportunities to enrich his work experience which stimulated him and renewed his energy. As leaders' profiles grow, they are also sought out by others, which is rewarding and motivating. Throughout one's career, that begins at a local level and over time, if one is lucky, it expands to an international level. International experiences cycle back to infuse more immediate work situations with energy and fresh ideas. Such experiences continue to renew Ernie's energy, and he is still, as always, cheered by talking with others, particularly library school students who themselves come with energy and ideas and a desire to make a difference. For Ernie, too, the desire to make a difference continues to compel him to put much of himself into his work.

## *Physical Well-Being*

The demands of library leaders are great—intellectually, emotionally, spiritually, and physically. Those involved in this project evenly indicated that their health has suffered or that it had not. About half reported a strong constitution and immunity system, and that they were in very good health overall. Because of demanding schedules, finding the time and perhaps more importantly, the energy to exercise, was difficult. Negative results of this may be compromised by physical strength and fewer opportunities to counter the impact of stress. Jo Bryant reported that the day-to-day stress, and that which occurs around certain times such as the budget process and labor negotiations, can drive her anxiety into overload. She tries to deal with this through deep breathing exercises, exercise, diet adjustments such as avoidance of caffinated beverages and drugs, although she does enjoy wine on occasion (as do many librarians in my experience). A number of the other leaders profiled here maintain regular workout routines, and some, such as Ernie Ingles, are engaging in highly active sports, such as downhill skiing.

Sleep disruption was reported by a couple of leaders, which includes disturbed sleeping time, awaking at early or odd hours, and for some, this tends to be an ongoing reality. A small number of leaders reported major health issues such as cancer, which cannot necessarily be attributed to their work, although one leader reported pre-ulcer and colitis issues due to stress. Another leader has, again because of a demanding schedule, used vacation time for major surgery and has had to work full-time through chemotherapy and radiation treatments since corporate managers insisted on reducing the number of sick days. Paradoxically, one leader noted that health has been impacted for good and ill: "I think that I have caused some damage to myself by pushing too hard. On the other hand, sitting around and doing nothing makes me sick for certain."

## *Summary*

The leaders profiled in this section are those many of us have come to know and respect throughout North America. They have served society, the profession, and each of us most broadly through their vision, passion, courage, tenacity, and integrity. In doing so, they have sought to balance work and family life, and also to reserve sacred time for themselves. We are lucky to have them, and luckier when we know them personally.

# Chapter Four

# How a Garden Grows: Nurturing Leadership through Educational Institutes

While the previous chapter is a profile of library leaders, this chapter is a rendering of ways in which we come to know such leaders and describes some of the opportunities the library community has created to meet these and other leaders, learn from them and develop ongoing mentoring relationships with them.

Warren Bennis (1997) believes that leadership can be learned, and that terrific coaches can create experiential opportunities to facilitate learning. He suggests that learning to lead is like learning to become a whole, integrated person, and that leadership coaches can play a pivotal role in personal transformation. The "rub," as Bennis puts it, is to be supportive and not controlling, and to give positive feedback without harming self-esteem. He claims that people learn about leading experientially, and learn through innovative learning opportunities that involve participation.

I have had the unique privilege of involvement with two highly supportive, experiential library leadership institutes in North America: Snowbird in the United States and Northern Exposure to Leadership (NEL) in Canada. I attended the Snowbird leadership institute in 1993, held annually in the Wasatch Mountains of Utah, upon the nomination of Margaret Andrewes, then President of the Canadian Library Association. NEL was started after my return from the United States and began in 1994; it is held every eighteen months at Emerald Lake Lodge near Field, British Columbia, Canada. Both Institutes are five-day, residential programs offering unique leadership education opportunities for new professionals.

Leadership themes typically include vision, risk-taking, creativity, interpersonal relationships, self-understanding, self-leadership, celebration, communication, organizational dynamics, and advocacy. These themes were selected based in part on similar leadership institutes and were deemed important by the programmers as well as library leaders. The themes were developed by the programmers, based on their own skills, interests, insights, passions, and preferences and have evolved over time. The institutes provide an opportunity for participants to hear from library leaders about these topics, and how the demands of each are balanced with those more personal. Library leaders are invited to participate as mentors and serve to facilitate group work as well as act as guides, coaches, and role models. In these ways, the programs have been ones that emanate from a profession coming to appreciate and benefit from its own leadership.

The programs are designed to be highly individual and personal opportunities for self-awareness and growth. They employ both experiential as well as direct delivery methods of teaching with a concentration on the former. They recognize that individuals learn in a multitude of ways, including those traditionally encountered, such as direct delivery, reading, and discussion, and also give participants the opportunity to learn by experience through activities and simulations, as well as group and individual work. The programs draw upon learners' histories, and address their real, immediate, and future concerns.

The Snowbird leadership experience was a special and unprecedented experience in which I felt a gestalt of respect, care, and quality. Rarely before had I been treated with such respect for my abilities and my person. Indeed, at Snowbird, I was treated as a leader, and in that sense, I was treated better perhaps than my abilities at the time would have warranted. By virtue of being nominated and selected to attend, I understood that from the perspective of colleagues and the Snowbird Institute, I was a leader, intelligent, and my contribution, both existing and potential, was highly valued. My person—not simply as a professional, but as a human being—was cared for. People cared about who I was, how I felt, and what I thought. And while I don't always recall now what I learned there, I do recall how I felt.

A gestalt of respect and care was exhibited in a tangible way through the quality of sessions as well as the quality of service. The Snowbird leadership institute was directed by the late Dennis Day of Salt Lake City Public Library. I am less familiar with the history of Snowbird than I am of NEL, and therefore, leave that accounting to those better versed in it than I, but given my intimate knowledge and participation with the development of NEL, I will offer a history of that here. Dennis Day, as the force behind Snowbird, offered encouragement to the creation of NEL. In doing so, he exhibited his grand and gracious manner, and modeled true leadership as someone who cared more for creativity in others than credit for self. As we created NEL, he advised us about administration, ethical concerns and program intent, and supported us in our bid to acquire funding. He sincerely cared for the profession, and in no way was proprietary about the successes he had achieved with Snowbird. Dennis was greatly assisted by Nancy Tessman, as well as the facilitators, Becky Schreiber and John Shannon. This effervescent couple contributed much to Snowbird. They had a quality of presence, of being in the moment, of extending great care, and of shining brightly that is rare in an individual, let alone a couple. Their personal spirituality added a special component to Snowbird, just as the spirituality at NEL is unique to the persons who created it. This aspect models the recognition that each participant is a full human being complete with spirit and soul, and honors that recognition. It is also indicative of the uniqueness that individual teachers bring to their work, and the distinct contribution that each makes. Another person who made this a special experience was Paul Sybrowski, then President of Dynix, Inc., who extended great personal kindness and generosity toward me, but more importantly represented a leader able to readily reveal his profound love and respect for his family. This revelation reminds us that one can lead well while being committed to family, and model that these two facets of life dialectically support and sustain each other.

Those involved with Snowbird paid attention to my needs, preferences and desires, listened to my concerns, cared for me, and took care of me. For example, they transported by some feat of magic, tables, chairs, white linen, candles, and china to the top of a mountain—simply to serve thirty or so new librarians dinner. They did this for us, and by inclusion, they did this for me. It was striking that someone would expend such energy on my behalf, and I was reminded of a poem by Judith Duerk (1993, p. 18) "How would your life have been different if there had been a place for you to go when your life was difficult . . . if someone had prepared a place for you?"

Experiential learning was also memorable. After completing eighteen years of formal education, the Snowbird Institute was the first time that I felt as though I were an integral and important part of the learning dynamic. Not only did my participation seem necessary and valued, but experiential learning afforded me a nearly unprecedented opportunity to engage with learning in a new way. I was able to internalize the material in a way I had done only minimally prior to Snowbird.

Upon return to my home institution at the University of Alberta, the Library Director, Ernie Ingles, noticed that I was walking somewhat taller than I had at the point of my departure for Snowbird five days prior—and for someone of my five-foot, two-inch stature, every fraction was discernible. In answering his query about my experience at Snowbird, I described what I believed to be among the defining and most important aspects of that experience. As I described Snowbird to Ernie, I said that we needed to do this in Canada, not really imagining that we actually would, never dreaming that he would take me at my word—and being a little aghast when he did. Who were we to do such a thing? How could we possibly? Little then did I really understand leadership, especially that of Ernie Ingles.

Complementing Mr. Ingles' leadership, the need for a leadership institute had been long recognized in the library community in Canada, and a number of individuals, associations and groups had been interested in launching such an initiative. That need was propelled by an information-driven economy supported by rapidly changing technology that threatened to leave librarians in its wake. Thus, within two years, NEL was launched, and maintains as a cornerstone the above concepts, but has become a uniquely Canadian experience designed by Canadian librarians.

Ernie began the process by inviting members of the library community to meet to discuss how a Canadian leadership institute might be achieved. Those individuals shared their ideas and passion, and contributed to what eventually became Northern Exposure to Leadership. A subset of that group ultimately became responsible for the design and delivery of NEL. It consisted of: Ernie Ingles as the Director, Pat Cavill, a private library consultant from Calgary, Alberta, Don Caplan, a private consultant, and myself, a librarian at the University of Alberta. Fran Trehearne, a human resources expert, also assisted. Ernie invited this group to work with him to create NEL. Subsequently, Karen Adams, Director, Library Services and Information Resources, University of Alberta Libraries, and Trevor Hamons, a private consultant, also became programming members. Ken Haycock, profiled in this book, leads a session on Myers-Briggs. Senior librarians volunteer their time to work with individual groups at the Institute itself, and serve as mentors.

Early in the process, a conscious decision was made to keep the Institute at arm's length from any formal body. NEL was designed to avoid a quagmire of well-intentioned, but policy bound organizations, committees, and boards. The construction of NEL is the result of a group of caring, impassioned, committed individuals, who informally, through discussions and professional feedback, seek and take counsel from the profession more broadly. The decision to design NEL in this way was taken to ensure that the team directing NEL had the autonomy, the freedom and the flexibility to set and pursue its defined vision, mission, and objectives.

The programs of the Snowbird Leadership Institute and Northern Exposure to Leadership shared some similarities, and also had the benefit of unique characteristics. Therefore, although this chapter is illustrative of both institutes, my greatest personal experience is with NEL and it is thus NEL that is the primary focus of this chapter.

## NEL Vision and Program

The vision of NEL specifically, is to contribute to the vitality, growth, and success of the library profession well into the twenty-first century by positioning professionals to be proactive, effective, and consequential voices in a dynamic and sophisticated information environment. The mission is to motivate professional librarians who have been identified as having leadership potential in order to assist them in developing, strengthening, and exercising their individual leadership abilities so that they are better prepared to create, articulate, and achieve organizational visions for the benefit of library service and society at large. The goals are to instill progressive and effective leadership strategies, attitudes and skills by:

- providing participants with an individual and personal learning experience in order to build a foundation upon which they can develop leadership skills;
- encouraging participants to recognize and initiate creative innovations and seize opportunity, especially when there is risk involved;
- guiding participants to appreciate and thrive in a changing political and demographic environment;
- encouraging participants to build individual networks; and
- affording the library profession a forum in which to begin to create a community of library leaders.

The program combines experiential and theoretical learning, with an emphasis on the former. The program:

- models leadership, group work, team building, and collegiality;
- engages participants in discussions about leadership, what it means, how it is recognized, developed, and sustained;

- exposes participants to a variety of leadership styles, including those that are innovative and may fall outside of traditional North American and European thought;
- provides an opportunity to learn from team-based approaches;
- offers participants an opportunity to develop, hone, and practice leadership skills;
- engages participants at an intellectual, soulful, spiritual and physical level; and
- recognizes that participants are whole human beings with roles and responsibilities other than those within the paid workforce.

The opening of the Institute is designed to give an overview of leadership, to discuss the desired outcomes of the experience, and to encourage participants to allow themselves to be open to what they will encounter. They are encouraged to, as much as possible, put biases and preconceived notions aside, and to participate in the sessions with a minimal degree of anticipation.

The first series of sessions develops self-understanding, and includes the Myers-Briggs inventory, which is intended to give participants an opportunity to develop an enriched understanding of themselves and their own leadership potential. It also relays the inherent message that participants are the point of departure for what is undertaken at the Institute, and that the Institute is designed to be a highly personal experience. The next session is designed to explore and increase the levels of risk they are willing or wanting to take. The final session gives participants an opportunity to brainstorm about their hopes, dreams and desires for their future as professional librarians, as well as reflect upon their vision for the library community.

The next series of sessions is called *Finding Passion, Courage and Vision.* These sessions are designed to have participants discover passion and courage as the basis for advocacy. They learn a model for advocacy planning, experience the visioning process, and learn a model for vision creation. This series has an evening of celebration, called the *Celebration Dinner,* which I created to involve participants, mentors, and facilitators so that each may share with the whole group something about themselves of which they are proud. They wear clothing to reflect that achievement to the dinner celebration, which may be a metaphor of the topic of their celebration. Typically, this is a colorful evening of rich sharing and a turning point of the Institute resulting in firmer group bonding and community building.

The next series of sessions is called *Coping with Change: Professional and Personal Perspectives.* The objective of this series is to help participants view change in a positive light and provide them with experiences and tools to help them understand change and transition. This section employs an organizational simulation activity called CHAOS, which portrays organizational dynamics.

The next series of sessions is called *Taking it Home: Living as a Leader.* The objective of this series is to have participants understand and be comfortable with how the theory and experience of the previous four days translates into real life. It is designed to assist them in developing an action plan to implement when they get home, and to discuss the issues that may arise as they make the transition or experience "re-entry" into their home and work lives. They are also provided the opportunity to meet with mentors and facilitators on a one-on-one basis in order to discuss any ongoing or outstanding issues, questions or concerns.

The final series is called *Reflections of Emerald Lake.* The objective of this series is to evaluate various aspects of the week, and to close on a positive note that blends learning, community, nature, and spirituality. Participants are not evaluated, which suggests that they are respected peers, accepted as they are, that their learning is their responsibility and the degree to which they learned anything at NEL is for them to determine. Of particular note in this series is an aboriginal sweet-grass ritual, which involves gift giving.

Overall, the key characteristics of this Institute include its residential learning context, as well as the profession-based nature of its creation, design, and delivery. A professional group of librarians saw the need to enhance leadership skills within the profession, and undertook to do so. The Institute is a forum in which librarians new to the profession can meet and interact with and learn from senior library professionals in a caring environment.

## The NEL Players:
## Participants, Mentors, Facilitators

NEL is designed for librarians who have graduated from a library school within the last seven years and have worked in a professional capacity for at least one year. Participants are those who meet these criteria and who have exhibited, in the opinion of nominators, leadership potential, as well as the ability to share with others their enthusiasm, positive outlook, and vision for library services of the future. Nominations are sought from employers, professional colleagues, associations, and library schools. Persons being nominated are asked to submit a short résumé and a one-page synopsis of achievements, career goals, and expectations of the Institute. Twenty-four participants are selected by a small committee and every attempt is made to either call or meet with potential participants prior to their being selected for the Institute. The intent of these meetings is to give participants some idea of the demands of the Institute, to learn more about their expectations of NEL, and to answer their questions.

The selection committee seeks to achieve the greatest diversity possible, and considers elements such as type of professional work, geography, and culture. It strives to include participants who represent all regions of the country, different nationalities, cultures, and first languages; socioeconomic status (and offers some financial support for those who need it); gender; type of library including academic, public, special, school, and government; and, type of work including reference, administration, collections, systems, and technical services.

Professional leaders are invited to serve as mentors. They participate voluntarily, which sets a tone of commitment, community, and collegiality. Mentors are friends and colleagues of the facilitators who openly share the ways they have maintained passion for their work and the efforts they extend to enrich and enhance each other's careers. Mentors have been librarians, consultants, and corporate executives, and rotate from year to year.

Ideally, mentors are willing and able to take risks; model leadership qualities; be fully present; exhibit good will and caring personalities; believe in the group process and the Institute; be open; be aware of their own preferences, biases, and approaches; be forthright in encouraging members to develop their own standards; exhibit personal power, stamina, curiosity, authenticity, and personal dedication; and have a sense of humor. They strive to listen more than they speak, reflect, clarify, summarize, empathize, question, link, support, model, suggest, and initiate as appropriate. Mentors engage in group discussions that provide them an opportunity to talk with participants about what has motivated, helped, hindered, and inspired them in their professional activities. Additionally, they typically share how they have balanced those activities with their personal lives. Mentors engage in daily discussions with facilitators about how the day's activities have gone, may seek advice on how to deal with any situations that may have developed, and offer suggestions for improvements. In a professional newsletter, one participant wrote:

> The mentors were extremely approachable and friendly. They worked alongside us in our respective teams. We shared these experiences with them, creating a unique bond. This closeness was important to me because I have never had the opportunity to have personal contact with leaders of the library profession. Usually, these people would have been out of reach for many of us. As I reflect on the words they spoke to us, I see more possibilities for my own career. I have a better idea of the direction I want to take, as well as what I need to accomplish along the way. (Franklin, 1996, p. 14)

Facilitators are responsible for designing and delivering the program, selecting participants and mentors, securing funding, making logistical arrangements, and promoting and arranging the Institute. For this group, preparation for the pilgrimage to

Emerald Lake Lodge is made well in advance. We embark on this journey ever and always full of anticipation, expectation, enchantment, and wonderment (if not a bit of anxiety).

The Institute employs a co-leadership model, which takes advantage of individual's specific area of expertise, allows for back-up if someone is sick or otherwise absent, provides participants the opportunity to experience a range and variety of facilitator styles, and allows the facilitators time to replenish their energy and prepare for subsequent sessions.

## The Soulfully Transformative Nature of NEL

*Those five days were pure magic. I will cherish the experience for a very long time.*

—Participant comment

*I was transformed by the experience, and my life has been changed.*

—Participant comment

*Many of the participants found the Institute both humbling and inspiring: humbling, because it broadened our perspective from our own work, our own type of library, our own worldview to glimpse the bigger picture of the profession and the Canadian library scene; and inspiring because we saw around us a group of keen, active, enthusiastic professionals. Participants and mentors alike commented on feeling refreshed, feeling a renewed optimism about the profession, and a renewed commitment to try to make a difference within it. We felt lucky to have been there.* (Haigh, 1995, p. 6)

*I believe I was touched at a soul level, while there.*

—Participant comment

*What I brought home with me is the following: a renewed commitment to the profession of librarianship; a sense of personal power; and a passion to contribute to this great profession.* (Franklin, 1996, p. 15)

*Most definitely, this has been one of the most profound experiences of my life so far.*

—Participant comment

The preceding comments from participants to NEL portray the profound impact that the Institute has had on the lives of the participants, the mentors, and the facilitators. Comments about NEL such as those above intrigued me, and I had numerous questions about them: What did people experience at Northern Exposure to Leadership? What inspired comments such as those above? What elements are perceived to be powerful enough to have moved people in this deep way, particularly at a soul level? If they were so moved, did this experience have a long-term effect on their careers or their lives? If so, how might that have happened? To begin to answer these questions, I embarked on doctoral research within the Faculty of Education at the University of British Columbia, Canada. Because I was in the Faculty of Education, I considered most fully what was to be gleaned from the Institute about adult education, as well as the relation of the soul to education.

Given the department within which I studied, my research was explored within an adult education framework, which is steeped in a rich tradition of creating caring learning communities that honor the histories of learners, listen to their individual voices, and allow for alternative ways of learning and knowing. My analysis and interpretation was set within a broader social context of individual, global, and cosmic alienation, and the demise and loss of soul evident in a manufactured, technical, and commodified world. This provided a rich context for my study that afforded interesting insights. While the former questions are answered within the context of this book, the latter questions dealing with pedagogy are more fully addressed within my doctoral dissertation itself (Brockmeyer-Klebaum, 2000). I will only briefly describe the methodology here.

Moore, in *The Education of the Heart* (1996a), argues that in its deepest forms, education is the art of enticing the soul to emerge from its cocoon or its cave of hiding to meet its potential. My research was about such enticement, and was an exploration of the intersection between education and soul and was intended to be a representative, fluid, and imprecise framework. It was not designed to be rigid, exact, or formulaic.

It was as a dance—with each reader, or dancer, choosing his or her own garb, pace, and melody. Similarly, this rendering of NEL is such a dance, and is the result of some of the choices I made in my research and as I reinterpret it as I write this book. Both my research and this chapter reflect my own ideas and application of literature and theory. Another researcher would have posed different questions, and created a different rendering of NEL. Therefore, it is not the definitive statement about NEL, but rather, one that reflected my own interests in soul as evidenced in—and elicited through— NEL.

The method of inquiry used in this research was primarily a qualitative approach, which is exploratory in nature and interpretive by design. This approach allowed themes, ideas, and concepts to emerge inductively from the research, and allowed me the flexibility to interpret the data outside of rigid guidelines. Employing an interpretive approach requires that the researcher makes interpretations to draw meaning from the data in order to enrich our understanding of events or processes. In this research, such interpretations were made at the level of interpreting the confluence of the collective of responses, and to a lesser degree, of the individual responses themselves. This investigation was intended to be descriptive in order to document and describe NEL; exploratory in order to identify important categories of meaning, and to investigate little understood areas of meaning; and, explanatory in order to identify plausible aspects shaping the experience (Marshall and Rossman, 1999, p. 33), all of which are accommodated with an interpretive methodology.

# NEL Research Results

Including the pilot and final surveys, 121 persons were surveyed; the response rate overall was 51.2% (62 respondents), which was considered respectable for my research purposes. Of those who responded, 17.7% (11 respondents) were mentors or facilitators and 82.3% (51 respondents) were participants. Also of those who responded, 64.5% (40 respondents) were female, and 35.5% (22 respondents) were male.

# The Gestalt of NEL:
## Its Soul, Its Emotion, and Its Spirit

What exactly happens at leadership institutes such as NEL eludes description, although one participant offered this analogy: "I remember the feeling of embarking on an adventure before I went and a feeling that I had had a momentous experience that I couldn't yet define when I left. Since then, I have likened it to losing your virginity—you feel changed but no one else can tell except maybe the others who were there."

Although it is difficult to describe, NEL has a powerful and profound impact on many, as the following participant noted: "When I got back home, I felt that I wanted time to process what had happened to me. I felt so tender and new, that the rough and tumble of every day was too much to bear right away . . . like I needed to grow another layer of skin."

Many respondents wrote about the rich and vivid memories they have of NEL, and described a very happy and fulfilling experience that was accentuated in a tranquil and beautiful setting where they met and spoke with peers and mentors in a caring and respectful environment. One participant noted: "My overall experience at Northern Exposure was one of the happiest times of my life. I have vivid memories of breathtaking scenery, fabulous food, stimulating discussions, wonderful people, and a shared understanding and respect—like a colorful patchwork quilt or tapestry."

Another participant draws attention to a number of elements that represent what the research identifies as key factors that influence soul in an educational environment. This comment highlights the aspects of personal growth, challenge, risk, and emotion, as well as ceremony and the sacred:

> I was moved or touched by the challenging things, the odd things, the funny things. Seeing my name on a card upon arrival at the airport and feeling important. Admiring the view from my cabin window. Wondering why I was out of breath after climbing only a few stairs to the Conference Centre. Discovering that I am an **** on the Myers-Briggs scale and being the only one like this in the whole group. Sitting down and hammering

out a shared vision statement for the profession with individuals from a variety of library environments. Reading the vision aloud in a fashion that bordered on drama. Crossing the line when asked a series of sensitive or difficult questions. Contemplating questions that might have been asked and thinking about how I would have responded. Listening to Robert Service poems high in the Rockies. Surviving a late night drive on a snowy mountain road. Walking along a mountain trail and reflecting on events happening in my life at the time. Sitting in a circle listening to Native voices. Finding it necessary to cry just at the moment when the pipe was passed to me and not really knowing why. Flying home on the same airplane with about eight NELlies all carrying blankets. Hearing a flight attendant speculate on whether there had been a sale on blankets. Sitting alone not really wanting to talk to anyone. Realizing that when I got home it was very difficult to explain to friends and colleagues what the whole NEL experience was about. Feeling somewhat pressured to act differently because of the experience. Accepting the fact that NEL was a significant event in my professional life.

Speaking more directly to what the foregoing participant mentioned, the next participant addresses directly the emotions that were elicited at NEL, and the nature of the environment as one in which emotions could be safely expressed:

I had a stop-over on my way home from Calgary. I had about an hour's wait and decided to call my sister. She asked me how "it" (NEL) was and all of a sudden I started crying. I think my emotional outburst really frightened her. I was a mixed-bag of emotions and needed to channel some of my feelings. I had a similar outburst when my husband picked me up at the airport. So NEL touched me, to say the least, on a very deep emotional level. The five days stimulated me on an intellectual level, but more importantly, I was inspired emotionally by my colleagues and mentors. The place was magical . . . the snow, the mountains, the seclusion and the food! Everything was incredible. I was touched by stories and inspired by others' experiences and passion, and grateful for the friendships that I made. The place was a spiritual haven. The ceremonies and rituals played an important part in my spiritual connections. I will not forget the blanket ceremony.

The totality of being moved at a soul level influenced learning about leadership very positively, as this participant noted:

> When you are touched at this soulful level you never ever forget it and therefore you learn more and remember more than you would in a traditional educational setting. I suppose it is the feeling of "passion" that makes the educational experience everlasting. We cared about what we were learning, because we were learning about ourselves. This caring is what made it the best educational experience ever.

These brief comments identify and articulate the unique and profound nature of the NEL experience. For the purpose of my research, the elements that impacted learning about leadership were: Human Factors: A Professional and Caring Community; Relationships with Mentors and Peers; Personal Growth; Celebration, Ceremony, and the Sacred; Risk; Struggle and Disclosure; Ethics; Creativity and Imagination; Physical Environment, Residential Factors; Impact on Life and Career; Teaching Methodologies; and Learning Through Soul. While all of these are discussed in the research mentioned earlier, only those focused on learning to lead within a community of leaders will be discussed here.

# Of Pageantry, People, and Places: Key Factors Impacting Soul

## A Professional and Caring Community Fosters Leadership and Inspires Hope

Kahne (1994) suggests:

> Democratic communitarians endorse societies in which members share commitments to one another and work together on common projects. They strive for free and full communication, social harmony, shared interests, scientifically informed debate, experimentation, and a sense of what John Gardner (1990) refers

to as a *wholeness incorporating diversity.* They seek to promote the support, sense of common mission, and sense of belonging that can come out of community and to avoid the envy, alienation, destructive competition, and exploitation that can result from the self-serving behavior of individuals. (p. 239)

Many of the community ideals noted by Kahne above were expressed in the responses to the NEL survey, particularly communication, shared interests, wholeness incorporating diversity, and a sense of belonging. These elements were supported by a key aspect of the soulfullness inherent in NEL that is building a caring community within librarianship. While part of the vision of NEL was the creation of a network, it seems to also be creating a community within the profession that is premised upon care. This factor represents a community of professionals at senior and junior levels, which binds the group and transforms the group into a community.

At NEL, senior and junior members of the profession meet, work together, talk, share ideas and stories, and build a network of colleagues. The role of mentoring and the use of workgroups are important in this process. This is similar to Delors' (1988) suggestion that education should be an expression of affection for people, whom we need to welcome into society. One mentor referred to this invitation as a rite of passage:

The most obvious thing I recall as a mentor at NEL was that my vocation as a librarian was affirmed in particularly arresting ways. I had always been a "dedicated leader" among librarians, but had not participated in the "rites of passage" as a professional that NEL entailed (that's because we didn't have such rites to honor our incoming generations before NEL). Nor had I fully appreciated the continuity of purpose, commitment, and philosophy with all types of libraries and all ages of librarianship, from ancient times to the present, until then, despite having a strong connection with the traditions of librarianship. What's my mission in relation to the next generation? I often think of the meetings I had with individual participants that last afternoon, when I began to see just how isolated, limited, and generally not honored most of the participants were in their work settings across the country. That led me to understand the role of senior library leaders in encouraging our next generation more clearly.

An invitation such as this by library leaders enhances commitment to the community, and in this case, to the profession of librarianship, as this participant noted: "The issues around leadership also reaffirmed my commitment to the profession of librarianship—I learned that change can be effected from within and that I owe as much to my organization as my profession." As Moore (1996b) suggests, those who serve community find that the extension of oneself can be enriching, inspiring, and thrilling. "Community makes the heart come alive and in that particular way brings charm and deep satisfaction to a person's life" (p. 121). A mentor observed:

> I realized that after some years of the soul-destroying cutbacks, downsizing and prevention of career advancement, I had inwardly become too pessimistic about the future of the profession in spite of often saying I couldn't afford the luxury of pessimism. After NEL, I became much more optimistic about our prospects. This optimism probably made it much easier to begin the planning for the conclusion of my own career.

The atmosphere is one in which the organizers and mentors participate for the purpose of service to the junior members of the group, in order to assist their learning, and help them to feel welcomed and respected within a professional community of colleagues. This participant appreciated being part of a professional community: "I very much get a sense that these people do form a community across the country and you see that when everybody comes together at CLA (Canadian Library Association Annual Conference), for example."

Even among mentors who already knew each other as colleagues, new depth was achieved among relationships with peers as well as with new professionals. This mentor appreciated getting to know colleagues better in a unique setting: "NEL has made it easier to see my place as an existing professional in a positive light, and connected me to emerging professionals in a way that cannot happen inside the workplace. It has also given me the opportunity to know my own colleagues better, and in a different setting."

The next participant found the drawing together of other professionals to be reinvigorating and encouraging, as this participant noted:

> I happily discovered that there are some very energetic, skilled people in the library and information field. I live in an area with few librarians and sadly, many of them could be classified as stereotypical librarians. While there is nothing wrong with this, for a young person in this profession it is disheartening to work with people who are not proactive about the programs and services that a library can provide. Often, they would rather just work in the status quo until it is time for them to retire. I found that I was encouraged by the people that I met at Emerald Lake and I had a renewed sense of purpose in my work.

The feeling of reinvigoration is also extended to how participants view others in the profession, and the profession itself. Some want to encourage others who advance the profession by promoting the services libraries offer, and by being a library advocate, as the following participant noted:

> I am proud to have been a participant in the first-ever Northern Exposure to Leadership, proud to have been nominated by my (then) supervisor. The whole experience contributed to my self-confidence, and my interest in, and dedication to, libraries. When involved in hiring now, I always ask myself if the candidate could be described as a library advocate, which is a concept I didn't really think about before NEL.

The Institute intends to develop participants' shared interests in and commitments to common goals, encourage them to experiment and to make space for all opinions, even dissenting ones, in order to foster leadership as well as personal and social growth. Participants are encouraged to engage critically, reflect, and work together to achieve collective or individually desired outcomes. An implicit group norm or expectation at NEL is that everyone is there to learn, to grow, and to participate. This is done in an environment that is focused on individual experience in an open, warm, trusting, and supportive environment. Group cohesion is formed, and it is expected that people conduct themselves in a manner that is respectful of others. The mentors' primary role is to facilitate group learning and to exhibit care and understanding toward the participants.

Caring is a key factor at NEL and an important dimension of community, leadership, and individual educational relationships. Nel Noddings, an educational researcher, supports the idea of caring within the learning construct. She describes a caring relationship as one characterized by engrossment where the caregiver has open, nonselective receptivity, or attention, for the cared-for. By engrossment, Noddings (1992) means to empty oneself of self-concern and see, hear, and feel what the other is saying. It seems that this element is present at NEL, and also that it is modeled, as Noddings advises, through the participation of the mentors. One participant observed: "One of the aspects that made the greatest impression on me at the time was that a group of well-established, high profile mentors should care enough about the future of librarianship in Canada to run and participate in such a program."

Another important aspect is not just that participants are cared for, but that they are taken care of. As the following participant noted:

> Knowing that everything was so well taken care of, and so enjoyable, let me get down to the business at hand. What had the biggest impact on me was the way we were treated—the way everything was done with excellence. It made me realize that I need to find an environment that really values excellence in a way that I don't feel I'm being valued right now. So it was that overall tone of excellence; everything started on time and ended on time and we were treated like royalty, basically.

This comment highlights the way in which people come to feel cared for and respected and the importance of that both within leadership education forums, but also within the workplace, as well as within a profession. Caring, in my view, enables a group to become a community, senior professionals to become mentors aside from bosses, peers to become friends, individuals to become leaders, ceremony to become spiritual, and place to become magic. This is well expressed by the next participant, who also highlights the importance of acceptance and the nonjudgmental nature of NEL: "The acceptance of the mentors and leaders was a palpable force that had a significant impact on me. The majestic, awesome beauty of Emerald Lake helped me to open and be receptive to positive statements from the leaders and mentors. Being in that setting with those people made me feel very much bonded with everyone present—part of a caring community."

While some felt a strong sense of community, and were inspired by it and embraced in it, others did not, as this participant reported:

> I have mixed feelings about NEL. While I have encouraged others to go to NEL, I have found that the NEL designation has become (in my opinion) somewhat snobbish or arrogant—that there is an elitism about it which I'm not sure I want to promote. Don't misunderstand me, I found NEL a good process and am really close friends with a number of the participants, but the dynamic of the NEL alumni is not what I would have hoped it would be. One of my friends recently commented that I was quite common because I rode the bus every day—and I suppose I am common in other respects and am uncomfortable in "elitist" surroundings.

Another participant characterized it metaphorically as "an old boys club": "While NEL is a special honor for those who attend, I wonder if it doesn't create an illusion of elitism among us and also appear to non-NEL participants that we are attempting to form an old boys club that excludes those who aspire to be leaders."

A criticism levied against the Institute in the survey responses by two persons is that the nomination and selection process, or the Institute itself, is elitist: only those who meet the criteria are nominated and selected to attend. Of those who are nominated, about 60% are selected. It remains undetermined how many are eligible in the country and therefore difficult to determine what percentage is nominated, although I suspect about 25% might be nominated. Unfortunately, while the Institute seeks to be inclusive, it simply cannot accommodate all who would like to attend.

The nomination and selection process seeks out individuals who have exhibited leadership potential in order to enhance and nurture that potential, and in order to further develop leadership skills. Yet, it implicitly suggests that those selected have been identified as leaders, or that they are leaders. In this, there is potentially a degree of self-fulfilling prophecy because when people are told that they are leaders, have training in that capacity and believe they are, they are more likely to become so. From this, two unresolved sets of questions arise: If *everyone* could attend, would they feel less exceptional and less like *leaders*? Given my earlier comments that I believe everyone is a leader in some capacity, I think this would not be the case. Other questions one might pose are: If everyone could attend, would the Institute ultimately be less effective? And, might the Institute have greater success in achieving its vision of leadership training and community building if the program were available to greater numbers? Might it be the case that if as many librarians as possible developed their leadership skills, the community of library users would more greatly benefit? These are interesting questions to consider and as yet remain unanswered.

Two respondents believed that there is a tension between the professional benefits of NEL and perpetuating privileged opportunity. While it is advantageous to welcome and guide new and even mid-career professionals, this can be critiqued as perpetuating the "old boys club" by sustaining an apparatus that maintains and reinforces privileged selection. On the other hand, comments such as the one by the following participant indicates that many, even those attending NEL, still may feel marginalized in terms of opportunity or advancement.

My résumé credentials are not mainstream, and my age and inability to relocate seem to be major stumbling blocks in my continuing in librarianship. Many jobs are being given to young graduates (and in [geographic location omitted], especially males) for their "energetic and modern approach." Yet for "a woman of my age" with my passions unconcealed, a history of varied careers, self-motivated learning style, and interactive personal approach, I feel overlooked and undervalued in my place of employment. I have heard similar stories from nurses and teachers—interestingly also "female" professions that give much lip service to the mature student, but little encouragement is provided in reality to support the new career. Previous experience and training is also not acknowledged unless they are degrees or other certified credentials. The harshest critics of the mature female student trying to (re-)enter the work force are their same-age, same-sex, and professionally well-established peers. These experiences have been very painful and disheartening.

In librarianship as elsewhere, many new professionals suffer in a rut of marginal employment or unemployment resulting from the large number of baby-boomers (loosely defined, those born in the 1940s and 1950s) who hold desired and favored positions, as well as because of the reduced budgets many libraries experience. There are also broader issues within librarianship, such as those faced in many professions and occupations, which are related to sexism, ageism, racism, and so forth. Because these tensions and biases exist, those associated with NEL and similar institutes must be ever mindful of ways and means to counter them. Overall, however, the results of my research indicate that the development of a professional community premised upon welcoming and care nurture the soul, and by extension, serve the profession well in its development of leaders.

## Relationships with Mentors

A closely related element to community is mentoring. "If mentors didn't exist, we would have to invent them," claims Daloz (1999, p. 17). Indeed, we have created them through myth and story and legend, and they have existed as historic figures. Mentorship (like leadership) has a long history. *Mentor* was a senior and trusted friend in Homer's *Odyssey*. Mentor, a chief council member of Ithaca, was asked by Odysseus to assume the role of godfather, and care for the son of Odysseus, Telemachus, while Odysseus went to fight the battles of Troy. Mentor does so, and later, possessed by the god Athene, the Greek goddess of war, helps Telemachus. Athene, through Mentor, helps to prepare the ship that Telemachus was to use by gathering food and friends, and later guides Telemachus away from danger as he seeks to find his father (Colum, 1918).

Throughout history, people and communities have met the need for renewal and sustainability through the use of mentoring. Mentoring has been a process in which to watch over and guide the young, to invite them to participate and to assist them to meet the challenges they encounter. Mentors:

> are suffused with magic and play a key part in our trans-formation, reminding us that we can indeed survive the terror of the coming journey and undergo the transformation by moving through, not around, our fear. Mentors give us the magic that allows us to enter the darkness: a talisman to protect us from evil spells, a gem of wise advice, a map and sometimes simply courage. But always the mentor appears near the outset of the journey as a helper, equipping us in some way for what is to come, a midwife to our dreams, a keeper of the promise. (Daloz, 1999, p. 18)

Sound mentoring within a profession, a career, or a life can sometimes be a primary factor in the course one takes, the leadership to which one aspires, as well as in the richness and satisfaction one enjoys. In many cultures, some now more past than present, this role was assumed by teachers, elders, grandparents or older relatives, and some religions ascribe this role to godparents or their counterparts. This can be done on a formal or informal basis, and can be achieved either by design or default.

In a profession such as librarianship, there is typically no formal process that results in a mentoring relationship. In some cases, library school students may be provided the opportunity to partner with working professionals, but this is usually on a short-term basis. Thus, many new and mid-career librarians do not have professional mentoring relationships. However, it is important to the success of many. Chatman (1992) found that mentoring in librarianship, as in other professions, is a major factor in sponsoring the directors for major library positions. Mentoring relationships provide opportunities for learning and sharing ideas and approaches, creating networks and forming contacts, and for recommending protégés for positional advancement. As described by one NEL participant, mentors can provide career advice: "The one-on-one sessions with mentors of your choice had the greatest impact on me. I presented each of three mentors with my personal work dilemma and asked them what their take was on it. Each of them responded the same way—I was in a no-win situation and had to look at a different option, in my case moving from the library to a teaching position, and I took their advice and it worked out great."

As noted by another, mentors can also be of great value just with a brief word or small compliment that is meaningful: "I was inspired by the mentors. Karen Adams, Ernie Ingles, Donna Brockmeyer, and Penny McKee, were the four people that touched me in some way—either by a compliment, words of encouragement, or by helping to unravel and understand some feelings inside of me."

While mentorship can be perceived as beneficial on one hand, mentoring can also be critiqued as perpetuating an elite or otherwise advantaged group. Much research is required to dismantle the paradoxes of mentoring, its benefits and its limitations.

Various types and levels of mentoring occur at NEL. One type is educational and is embedded in the learning groups. In the learning groups, two mentors work with the participants throughout the five days. In this process, the mentoring is educationally focused, rather than career focused. This occurs on a group-to-group basis, as well as on an individual basis. Another type of mentoring is career or professional mentoring which also occurs at two levels. At one level, individuals are mentored on a one-on-one basis, as this participant noted: "My one-on-one meetings with the mentors/facilitators meant a lot to me. This probably has something to do with the fact that I'm most comfortable talking to one person at a time. I enjoyed the insights and observations that these three people, who I deeply respect, offered."

At another level, there was an overarching feeling of mentorship offered by the group of senior librarians to a group of junior librarians. As noted by this participant: "I was touched that such important people would take the time to organize and carry out an Institute." Another noted:

> The guides and mentors were obviously very emotionally invested in the Institute, and that feeling stays with me. I remember being met at the airport by Tom Macdonald, of Dynix. I was not expecting to be met, but thought I would find a sign pointing me in the right direction. Being met was a nice beginning. I also remember being driven here and there throughout the Institute by the guides and mentors, which gave everything a very personal feeling. I remember feeling, and still feel, that one day I would like to contribute similarly in such a dedicated fashion. They seemed to support each other well as a group, and I would love to belong to such a supportive work group someday.

Although this type of group-to-group mentorship is not the focus of much of the literature on mentorship, this framework was important to those who attended NEL, and warrants further study. Mentorship of this nature becomes important to the development of leadership in community at the group level, and by inclusion, at the individual level.

The previous comment also illustrates that participants appreciated the attention, care, and consideration of "high profile leaders" and this instilled in them confidence in their own abilities. Mentors appreciated the opportunity to "give something back," gained hope and faith that the future of the profession was in good hands, and sometimes felt they received as much as they gave.

Over the course of the five days, individual participants meet and talk with senior librarians, which may also be extended into ongoing mentoring relationships once NEL has ended. Participants and mentors alike are encouraged to seek out those short and long term relationships which can be rewarding for both. One point that was mentioned concerned the ongoing and regional lack of mentoring that participants experienced upon return to their places and regions of work.

The lack of mentoring has problematic implications. A small number of respondents indicated that they felt pressure as the result of NEL to assume leadership roles, and achieve success when doing so, or were worried that they might raise expectations that they couldn't meet. As this participant described:

> Over time, I continue to be interested in leadership and to evolve and refine both my skills and my understanding . . . sometimes it seems like so much more than I could ever attain . . . other times I catch myself doing something really good and think okay, that's what it's about . . . there is sometimes a real struggle to maintain a sense of how you can be a leader in your own organization . . . I realize that some of the initiative rests with me but I also think that it rests with organizations to foster and mentor . . . something that doesn't always happen. Although I know that I could really use regular mentoring and several of the NEL mentors are in ****, I haven't really pursued that . . . I think that I am afraid of raising expectations that I couldn't meet . . . I don't know where some of those folks get their energy and I know I don't have as much and I don't want to be in a position where I feel I am making excuses for being less of an achiever.

This comment has a number of issues embedded within it concerning the ongoing struggle of assuming leadership positions, and meeting or failing to meet the expectations that some perceive others have of them. Ongoing, post-Institute mentoring may address some of these issues.

At the end of each NEL day, an hour is dedicated to story-telling in a series of sessions called Northern Reflections. These sessions are an opportunity for each mentor to share with participants a candid and heart-felt portrayal of the experiences, challenges, triumphs, and values that shaped and directed their careers, and the ways in which they coped with the tensions of balancing home and family with active and engaging work lives. One participant appreciated a discussion about how to balance work and family responsibilities, for example: "I was literally

moved to tears when a mentor was talking about struggling with
the isolation that she had faced and trying to balance her family
and her career. She said that she couldn't find the answers for us
but that we have to keep working on that. That very much spoke
to a point that I am at in my life right now."

Another clearly appreciated the comments about the
importance of balance: "Quite frankly, the men's [stories] were
dull, dull, dull. But listening to the women made me remember
that work is squeezed into life, not the other way around. Kids
have to be raised, mortgages paid. The power of life lies not in
the career but in what happens outside of it."

The Northern Reflection series of sessions has been very
useful for all concerned with NEL. It represents a lens through
which listeners can view, assess, interpret, and more fully
appreciate and understand their own careers and lives. Stories,
Witherell and Noddings (1991) share, "attach us to others and to
our own histories by providing a tapestry rich with threads of
time, place, character, and even advice on what we might do
with our lives" (p. 1). As this participant noted:

> I had the chance to reflect on why I feel like I am in such a hurry
> for everything good to happen to me professionally. The
> Northern Reflections sessions were such an insight into the
> professional and personal experiences of the mentors that served
> to give me the message "slow down and listen." Why did I think
> that I could accomplish a lifetime of service and recognition in
> seven years? Who made me feel that that was an expectation?
> Why was I beginning to feel like I would be failure without a
> "marked" achievement or accomplishment? These sessions gave
> me an incredible opportunity to see what was realistic over a
> lifetime career—and these were extraordinary careers!

Northern Reflections was also a means through which the
participants come to see the mentors as "just people" and helps
the participants to ascribe "human faces" to those whom
otherwise might have been considered a distant and remote
leader within the profession. One participant shared: "Having
the faculty and mentors tell personal stories I found very
moving. It opened these leaders of our profession and gave them

human faces, and made me very appreciative of the sacrifices that they had made to become leaders." Another added that, with human faces, mentors were not so unlike the participants, and the resulting association may inspire participants to believe that they too could create dreams and reach them: "The Northern Reflections were inspiring. So many different paths blazed and roads followed . . . very interesting to listen to people you respect and admire only to discover that they are just 'ordinary' folks, like you. That you can accomplish as much and make a difference by seizing or creating opportunities, taking risks, and following your dreams."

The "human face" also aided group bonding and trust. Another participant appreciated the honesty of the stories and commented upon the way in which they can result in greater group bonding: "I enjoyed the honesty of the mentors. There was personal risk for them in the process of sharing with us stories of their personal and professional lives. That honesty brings a group closer together quickly." Similarly, another appreciated what they termed self-disclosure, and this resulted in trust: "I enjoyed the insights and observations that these three people whom I deeply respect offered. I also found the disclosures of particularly my team-mates and mentors to be quite evocative— the intimate sharing of experiences between new friends and the trust that was imparted with it."

For the storyteller, telling their stories is an opportunity to pause and reflect upon their own histories, how they have evolved, the meaning they have had, and the way in which the storyteller may want their histories to inform their futures. Cooper (1991) suggests: "Telling our own stories is a way to impose form upon our often chaotic experiences and in the process, to develop our own voice. Listening to our own stories is a way for us to nourish, encourage, and sustain ourselves, to enter into a caring relationship with all parts of our selves" (p. 97). As one mentor commented: "One of the most memorable moments for me was deciding what 'fireside' account of myself to give."

The Northern Reflections sessions contribute to the creation of community that forms at NEL, and validates other ways of knowing and making sense of our work and personal lives. It adds a dimension that joins "the worlds of thought and feeling, and [stories] give special voice to the feminine side of human experience—to the power of emotion, intuition, and relationships in human lives. They frequently reveal dilemmas of human caring and conflict, illuminating with the rich, vibrant language of feeling the various landscapes in which we meet the other morally. Through the poignant grip of story and metaphor we meet ourselves and the other in our mutual quest for goodness and meaning" (Noddings and Witherell, 1991, p. 4). This is well portrayed by the anecdote of one participant:

> I remember the storytelling. At the dinner where everyone celebrated themselves, Holly told a story. It was an oral tradition story about a wolf and a child. I thought that was just marvelous. I returned from the Institute and I hadn't seen my son in five days—he was a year and a half old. The first thing I did was grab him and hug him and we played a bit and then I told him that story. He was lying on his back and I had never told him an oral story before—I read to him from books. That story had lots of noises, pitter-patter (hands patting on knees) and shouting and moving around. I toned it down for the baby and he loved it and he was mesmerized. That really impacted me. I'm not a children's librarian and I would never have thought to do anything like that. It was a wonderful experience. I told Holly about that last night and she was thrilled. And it even brought tears to my eyes—it was not something I would have done before the Institute.

## Relationships with Peers

The foregoing anecdote illustrates the strong and meaningful bonds created among participants in workgroups. NEL uses work groups of eight people, which remain constant throughout the five days. Dirkx's research and writing discusses the relationship between the use of groups in educational settings and soul. He suggests that we recognize the person sitting in the present group, participating in the discussion, but that we also observe this adult learner as a child, a member of a family, a youthful learner in high school, or a hurt child chosen last for volleyball. We become conscious of these images, with a mixture of fondness and pain, and the two extremes seem to tug at the edges of our awareness (Dirkx, 1997). One participant simply proclaimed: "I loved all of the people in my group by the end of it."

Dirkx (1997) suggests that soul beckons us to a relationship between an individual and his or her broader world, and our emotions and feelings are languages that help us learn about relationships, the world, and our place in it. How we make sense of ourselves and others are critical aspects of learning. This connects the heart and mind, and mind and emotion, as we focus on the concrete and the present, which deepens the understanding of the meaning of learning in adulthood. Learning about where individuals fit into the world, based on their own needs and preferences can be elicited through group interaction as we gain insight through how others see us, as this participant noted:

> During our risk-taking session I shared my risk and revealed how much I want to get out of my job and move on. Through a process of discovery with both mentors in my group and with the participants in my group I was able to see that the need to leave was not coming from where I had originally defined it to be. The process of confronting that issue and coming to terms with what I needed to do to move forward and be happy was extremely painful but very necessary. Had I not undergone this process I would surely have left and still not come to terms with what was really at stake. I would in the end have been haunted by it.

Taylor (1997) suggests "It is through relationships that learners develop the necessary openness and confidence to deal with learning on an affective level, which is essential for managing the threatening and emotionally charged nature of the transformative learning experience" (p. 53). A number of respondents indicated the importance of relationships within their workgroups, both with other participants and with mentors. A mentor noted: "Maintaining the same group through the week was excellent because there was daily improvement in communication and in the group dynamic. It was fascinating to watch the individuals who were reticent at the start of the week unfold as the week progressed, clearly demonstrating a level of trust." The strength of group bonding was evident, and a formal representation of that depth was noted as important by this participant: "I remember being asked to take off our nametags at a certain time. I liked that. I liked that we agreed to wear them consistently until that time. It was a good way for people to work on the process of remembering names—a skill that is useful in all aspects of our lives. It also gave a strong message. We were no longer strangers."

Group bonding occurred at the individual group level as well as at the broader group level. Although it could be expected that NEL would provide an opportunity for networking, it is clear that it has become, for some, much more. The intensity and the depth of sharing both within groups and with roommates have resulted in interpersonal connections that were characterized as friendship. Although these relationships may not be actually maintained over an extended period of time, they are part of participants' memory, and influence the resonance of the Institute. One participant wrote: "The moments I tend to think of most frequently are the informal ones spent with friends that I made there. I had a lot of fun during those informal, nonallotted times. Similarly, another added: My fondest memories are of working with my small group. These were—are—great people and we had lots of laughs."

The next participant observed that perhaps not all of the activities and discussions in the working groups went smoothly all of the time, but despite interpersonal differences, the group worked through difficulties: "I remember how surprised I was at how well my working group got along. There were one or two groups that year which could not seem to reach a consensus on any issue, but our group seemed fairly cohesive, and able to work well together, in spite of some personal differences that arose. I enjoyed working in that group, being part of a team."

It is the practice at NEL to encourage groups to work through difficulties that may arise from time to time. As suggested by Dirkx (1997), this type of approach, rather than teachers or facilitators attempting to resolve differences, honors the soul of the group as well as its members. The use of productive work-groups can also serve as a model of leadership practice that can be transferred to the workplace. As noted in the description of NEL, modeling is an important teaching element at the Institute because it is more easily remembered and transferred to situations outside the Institute. The following participant used a workgroup activity in the workplace: "I liked the creation of ground rules. I have used this idea with the library staff in different ways, mostly subtle. Using this with a combination of humor has helped us deal as a group with difficult people and situations in ways that were productive and not hurtful. There are no surprises this way."

Another participant found a particular session that modeled diversity particularly useful in the workplace:

> The biggest frustration at my workplace was that all the older people I worked with were expecting me to bring them up to speed with the Internet and computers. I was frustrated because they were not taking initiative to learn themselves. I felt that they were putting an incredible burden on me, and I was actually starting to feel very resentful toward them. But during Fran's session on diversity, I noticed that some of the mentors admitted that they felt computer illiterate. I started to view my coworkers in a different light. I actually felt honored that I could contribute to their education in some way. I felt that instead of it being a job, I actually had something to contribute. For me, that was the starting point of shedding my negative feelings toward my coworkers and I realized that I was important.

The working groups at NEL were a means through which greater understanding and tolerance of, as well as appreciation for, others was achieved, which is a primary aspect of leadership. In many cases, strong bonds were formed, and friendships made. Group work also added an opportunity for enhanced self-understanding and personal growth, which was also an important element at NEL that moved deeply those involved.

# Relationship with Self

Leader, know thyself. NEL had an overall effect of being a personalized experience in which respondents reported a greater understanding of and appreciation for their own abilities which had the overall effect of improving self-confidence and self-esteem. Personal strengths, accountability, growth, and self-leadership were accented at NEL and occurred through a number of sessions, as well as through the program as a holistic unit.

Early in the program, elements of understanding personal preferences are addressed through the use of the Myers-Briggs Type Indicator tool. As well, individual and community visions are designed and individual plans of actions are developed for implementation when participants return home and to their workplaces. Taken together, the program and the overall tenor of NEL resulted in participants achieving personal growth, self-leadership, and personal direction. This participant shared: "I think that the most critical thing that happened to me at NEL was that of personal growth. I became more in touch with myself as a result of my participation. I have always had a problem with self-confidence in my professional life but I feel that as a result of what I learned at NEL, I grew in terms of my leadership potential."

This too was observed and believed by one of the mentors: "The opportunity the program offers to take quantum leaps in personal development was important. Compacted into that one week is a microcosm of what many of us have struggled through over a period of maybe 10 to 20 years. People who are intellectually and emotionally open can gain understandings from NEL that might take years to acquire otherwise."

The affirming experience of NEL begins at the initial nomination stages. For some, support from supervisors or others who may have nominated them gave participants greater confidence within their workplaces, and also enhanced self-esteem, as this participant expressed: "The fact that I was selected by my library and by NEL to go at all was a confidence booster and an indication of what my bosses thought of me and my work, and perhaps of how others outside the library perceived me and my potential." Being thought of as a leader, identified as a leader, and being selected to develop leadership skills positively influenced the way participants thought of themselves. This was the result not only of the nomination and selection process, but resulted from the topics explored at NEL.

Through the program elements, but also through the nature of NEL itself, NEL was a soul enriching affirmation of self. All involved were held in high regard. One way in which this is done, such as that suggested by Belenky et al. (1986), was through the recognition of the uniqueness of each individual. Through attention to the voices that arise from within, as compared to relying heavily on those from without, people felt affirmed. As noted by one respondent: "I felt a new sense of empowerment. I felt that my voice counts and is worth listening to." Those teaching leadership skills are generally aware of the importance of personalizing educational experiences as a means through which we can attend to the soul of individual persons. In hearing their voices as learners, educators model the esteem in which they hold students, which thereby enhances the esteem in which students then hold themselves. This participant made that direct observation: "The most moving, impacting aspect of NEL for me was the experience of being treated like a peer by the leaders and mentors. Throughout the conference, these people communicated in countless ways the message that they thought I was worth investing in; they believed that I could become a leader in the library profession."

The totality of environment, place, general tenor and treatment are alluded to in the following participant comment:

I believe having gone to NEL instilled more confidence in me—a greater calmness in the face of constant change and adversity—something I'm finding I need and use as I take on more significant leadership roles in my job. I don't think much of what was delivered at NEL was groundbreaking or original, rather, it was the way in which it was delivered that gave it so much impact.

Personal growth can be explicated by exploring some of the specific sessions that assisted mentors and participants in greater self-understanding and self-direction. One of those sessions employed the Myers-Briggs Type Indicator, which is a personality inventory tool. Respondents answer a set of questions by recording their preferences or approaches and are scored on a scale concerning Introvert or Extrovert, Intuitive or Sensing, Thinking or Feeling, Judging or Perceiving. This tool was used to give participants an opportunity to more fully understand themselves as well as appreciate that there are distinct and identifiable differences between human personalities. While they might know this at a cognitive level, this session provided an opportunity for participants to explore that idea while discussing specific differences through an interpretation of their own preferences and those of others within their groups. Generally, people understand that not every person has similar thoughts, opinions, preferences, and feelings, but still often assume others are much like they are. The Myers-Briggs Type Indicator highlights that not all people are the same, and is useful in understanding, adjusting to, and managing the differences. This participant appreciated both opportunities for growth: "It is always great to learn about oneself and reactions as well as those of others. It helps me deal with situations of potential frustration and anger and helps me see so much more in others."

Understanding self and drawing on inner wisdom is an important concept for soulful action. People are sometimes, I think, wiser than they, or others, know. It is sometimes the case, for example, that when we encounter an important idea, we might think "I knew that" and believe that the speaker or teacher, for example, is reminding us of an inner wisdom. We do know much, and paradoxically, we know little. Listening to inner voices and inner wisdom is a soulful approach to leading. When we feel we know little, I believe we can then draw upon our personal resources to guide us. Each individual has a source of personal power—it might be a sense of humor, an ability to calm stormy waters or the ability to inspire others to participate. Whatever our strengths, it is good to use them, and leaders should be encouraged to do so. One participant wrote in a professional journal:

> When Donna Brockmeyer-Klebaum was speaking about leading yourself, I realized I do not have to be a CEO of a library in order to be a leader in my profession. Through my experience, I have found "personal power" to create change because ultimately, the power for change lies within the individual. At NEL we discover that a leader is not someone who will necessarily be a CEO; a leader is someone who can make a difference in their profession by bringing energy, passion, and vision to their workplace. A leader is someone who leads themself first. (Franklin, 1996, p. 15)

Self-leadership at NEL was also considered through a personal and individual action planning session in which participants, building on their own strengths, and drawing from their own objectives and desires, create a plan of action for implementation upon their return home. This participant noted:

> Most people want to learn more about themselves and their approaches which helps them respond better to change. The program that is offered does this. I think the action planning at the end was very valuable with participants identifying long-term commitments. I believe that components such as *Leading Yourself* are particularly important elements of the overall experience.

Some of the mentors also made strong assertions of personal growth, exemplified in this comment:

> I attended my first NEL pretty much as just another speaking gig. While I assumed there would be changes in the participants I did not expect there to be significant changes in any of the mentors and the like. By the end of the session I had undergone several changes for the better. I can also state on a very personal note that elements of the final healing circle in NEL (a totally new experience for me) moved me deeply on a number of levels and led me upon my return to a serious attempt to salvage a failing marriage. While it was not salvaged, because of the

change in me things were able to be said and things came out that made the eventual parting humane and non-corrosive. I believe the ritual, particularly the inherent neutrality and "forgiveness" of aboriginal ritual was an important element in opening participants to change.

Because NEL is a highly personalized educational opportunity, there is potential growth and human connection for all involved. Human relationships with peers, mentors and self were among the most important and key factors that moved deeply and at a soul level those involved, and added much insight into their own leadership.

## Residential Factors:
## Bunking in and Breaking Bread

The relationships that participants formed with themselves and each other was enhanced by the environment both in terms of residence learning as well as physical environment.

Fleming (1998) found in her research that residential learning had a strong impact on relationships with others. She notes:

> Participant descriptions of relationships reflected the differences they perceived between developing relationships in residence and in their normal lives. In particular, they noted an association forms among a group of people that is different from that which is normally possible in a traditional classroom. Participants used terms such as *fellowship, togetherness, community*, and *family* and referred to the formation of a *cohort, group cohesion,* and the *coalescing of groups.* (p. 264)

She found that the residential factor was a "necessary dimension for creating significant interpersonal relationships" (p. 264) given the limited amount of time. A number of key elements were identified as influencing the nature of the relationships, and could be claimed to have impacted the relationships that formed at NEL as well. Two include shared sleeping quarters and dropping facades. One participant wrote:

I was moved when my group met at a member's room and we talked about why it was we became librarians in the first place. I was moved to discover that my fellow group members had become librarians for some of the same reasons I had. I felt a real sense of community and a connection to these people whom I had known for only a short time and this for me was a spiritual experience.

Those involved also dropped their facades of professional titles, roles, behaviors, and relationships formed between those who would not normally meet because they crossed rank. This also may lend support to the belief that issues of power and rank are less an issue at NEL than they may be in other contexts. A participant noted: "The opportunities to socialize at meal times and in the evenings was important. Playing various snooker games with Paul, Ernie, Ron, Richard, and Louis was an opportunity to sort of step outside of NEL for a few moments and just hang out."

Those involved with NEL also shared meals. While food feeds the body, it also nurtures the soul. In an educational setting such as NEL, mealtimes provide an opportunity to sit and relax and become acquainted with colleagues. The dining room at Emerald Lake is elegant, but cozy and informal. The furnishings are as one would expect in a rustic but upscale mountain lodge. The lighting is soft and the windows admit the mountains and lake. The early guides at Emerald Lake came from Switzerland, Austria, and Germany. They learned from the local First Nations people to cure and smoke game and fish, gather seasonal berries, and forage for root vegetables. This early means of sustenance evolved into the cuisine offered today.

Meals begin with a basket of bread. Bread has an ancient and rich tradition associated with symbolism and the sacred. The discovery of bread ovens in ancient goddess shrines dating back to 7200 B.C. indicates there may have been a sacred bread tradition in which the oven represented the womb of the goddess (Redmond, 1997, p. 46). Bread appears later in many ceremonies and religions, as in Christianity as the body of Christ and as a means to feed masses. It also represents transformation: grain to flour to dough to bread. This is symbolic of leadership learning: from potential, support, and training to performance.

Souls in general, and those of leaders have been described as existing in the depths of persons at their very core. The root vegetables offered at Emerald Lake Lodge inspire, if only viscerally, a sense of grounding, and of the earth. Miniature beets, white turnips, purple onions, small red potatoes, and baby carrots are soul food. So too, is the cornucopia of wild mushrooms: porcine, chanterelles, morels, puffballs, lobster mushrooms, and pine mushrooms, which evoke images of the mossyness of soul. Much of the food served in the dining room is unprocessed and close to the earth: wild rice, squash, flowers, herbs, spices, berries, lentils, as well as wild game and fish, sometimes cooked in birch bark.

During the Paleolithic era, when meat was a staple, tribes lived in a symbiotic relationship with animals. Cave paintings, preserved in chambers deep within the earth, depict a mystical human-animal relationship, rather than a glorification of the hunt (Redmond, 1997). Taken together, foods such as these potentially remind us of the earth in a direct, inter-relational way, rather than one distanced by processing and packaging, and one of symbiosis and honoring rather than presuming and consuming. This grounded, holistic environment is a sound and strong foundation from which to lead that reminds those present that we are stewards of a physical place that must be cared for and nurtured as our physical world nurtures human beings.

In summary, sharing accommodations and meals allowed participants to become closer, more comfortable with each other, and more open. It also allowed groups of people (such as seniors and juniors in the profession) to mix in a relaxed way (chatting, playing pool), which reinforces and inspires leadership.

## Physical Environment: The Place of Pan

"A cry went through late antiquity: *Great Pan is dead*!" Pan, in Greek mythology, was a nature-god, a rustic god, or a wood spirit. He is sometimes depicted as half man and half goat with horns, a beard, and tail. His body is completely covered with fur. He lived in woods and caves, traversed the tops of mountains, and protected flocks of sheep. In Plutarch, he is pronounced dead, and given that his death coincides with the birth of Christ, it is sometimes believed that this signifies the end of an old world, the birth of a new one.

This captures the sentiment that nature had become deprived of its creative voice and its independent living force of generativity; its soul as well as our psychic ability to connect with nature, were lost. With Pan dead, Hillman suggests, so too was Echo, a nymph beloved by Pan, who could only reflect what she heard. Hence, humans could no longer capture consciousness by reflecting within their natural instincts.

> Nature no longer spoke to us—or we could no longer hear. The person of Pan the mediator, like an ether who invisibly enveloped all natural things with personal meaning, with brightness, had vanished. Stones became only stones—trees, trees; things, places and animals no longer were this god or that, but became *symbols* or were said to *belong* to one god or another. When Pan is alive, then nature is too and it is filled with gods. (Hillman, 1989, p. 97)

Of course, who is to say that Pan is dead? Perhaps Pan is repressed, as Hillman suggests. And how might we release or awaken Pan within leadership opportunities, and for what reason? To awaken Pan may well be another way to nurture leadership potential and strengthen leadership action.

A magical physical environment is the site of NEL, which is held at Emerald Lake Lodge, near Field, British Columbia, Canada. While Emerald Lake is secluded and serene, it is relatively easy to reach, located just 10 kilometers off the TransCanada highway, two hours from Calgary, Alberta. It is indeed an amazing site, as expressed by this participant: "I will always remember the beauty of the mountains—the scenery was so awe-inspiring and so peaceful that I knew something wonderful was going to happen the moment I walked into the resort area."

The main lodge emerges from the landscape in hand-hewn logs constructed in 1902 by the Canadian Pacific Railway. It graces the shores of the still and shimmering Emerald Lake, the color of which reflects its name, and sits on a small peninsula reachable by a footbridge. Since 1902, renovations have realized a beautiful main lodge that is unpretentiously elegant and welcoming. Inside, a curved stair leads to two session rooms with windows to the mountains, adjacent areas for quiet conversation, relaxation, or reflection, and to a game room with an antique billiards table, chess boards, and a piano. The guest cabins are beautifully appointed with willow furnishing and down duvets, and are replete with wood-burning fireplaces and private balconies. The facilities were appreciated by this mentor: "The general ambience touched me at a soulful, spiritual level. Being able to light a fire, slide under a sumptuous duvet, and gaze out at snow-topped firs, Christmas lights, and a dark sky straight in front, with the fire dancing just a bit to the right was sheer delight."

Although Emerald Lake has down duvets and great fieldstone fireplaces and an open shoreline fire pit, the enchantment is also in what it doesn't have. There are no closely accessible restaurants or shops, no televisions or radios or traffic noises (unless you're there at the same time as a German film crew), few computer outlets, and no cell phone transmitter stations. The seclusion and relative silence offers an increasingly rare opportunity for reflection and contemplation. The focus and reflection this type of environment offers is instrumental for leadership education to permeate to deeper levels which increases opportunities for internalization. This environment attends to the soul, which enhances learning. As Moore (1996b) suggests:

> Silence is not an absence of sound but rather a shifting of attention toward sounds that speak to the soul. In a moment of silence you may feel your heartbeat or hear your breathing. Silence is a positive kind of hearing, which requires turning off the knob that tunes in to active, literal life and turning on the one that amplifies the movements of the soul. (p. 105)

In another work, Moore (1996a) writes: "Sometimes the spirit of a place is so strong you may think you see its face and glimpse it gamboling over a field or peeking out of a forest, but at other times you struggle for words to describe it" (p. 145). The power of the spirit at Emerald Lake persuades its visitors that gods live there. As one draws breath, a living force takes residence; such a presence engages the soul in ways that sterile or bleak environments cannot.

Many North Americans are appreciating the value of spirituality and nature. They create refuges alongside lakes, streams, and oceans, and in the mountains. Eco-tourism is becoming extremely important to many, which could be argued to be a kind of soulful or spiritual recognition of and respect for the natural environment. In great measure, we want Pan alive. "When Pan is dead, then nature can be controlled by the will of the new God, man, modeled in the image of Prometheus or Hercules, creating from it and polluting in it without a troubled conscience" (Hillman, 1989, p. 97).

Nature should be honored and respected. Like little else, it has the capacity to humble, as well as to inspire. I sometimes say that in Saskatchewan, my home province, one can die in a day— either from exposure and hypothermia in the winter or exposure and dehydration in the summer. On the other hand, the skies are alive with the color of sunset during harvest and the sound of gathering geese in the fall and a musky odor permeates the senses to draw one into the earth. So, too, does the natural element at NEL both humble and inspire. The mountain peaks and scree slopes are distant and massive and cold. We know they are deadly, even though we may feel safe, as in the poem *David* by Earle Birney (1959):

> *That day we chanced on the skull and the splayed white ribs*
> *Of a mountain goat underneath a cliff, caught tight*
> *On a rock, Around were the silken feathers of kites.*
> *And that was the first that I knew a goat could slip.* (p. 349)

If mountain goats can sometimes slip, so, too, can leaders. And of course, in the majesty of this, we are tiny and sometimes frail. Yet, while that is true, we are also inspired and gently held.

The nature gods serenade us to be big. The mountains sit with ease so tall that they inspire us to be gracious and open in thought and deed and vision. They are young and craggy with shards like fractured crystal, because they have not had the eons of weather to round their reaches, as have other, older mountain ranges. In that, they reflect the new librarians who attend NEL: both are ungroomed, perhaps impetuous and critical, but sharp and brilliant and strong.

The trees belong there, and through their belonging offer comfort so that we, too, feel we belong. The Roman philosopher Seneca observed, "If you came upon a grove of old trees that have lifted their crowns up above the common height and shut out the light of the sky by the darkness of their interlacing boughs, you feel that there is a spirit in the place, so lofty is the wood, so lone the spot, so wondrous the thick unbroken shade" (Cousineau, 1994, p. 160). Such it is at Emerald Lake. You feel there is a spirit of the place, which is what many cultures through history have believed of trees. It was recently suggested to me by a Cree woman that I "go into the woods and put down some tobacco, or hang prayer flags. Talk to the trees. They will listen to you; they were people once." Too, the truly emerald waters lap at the shores of our consciousness and speak for our peace, and of magic and mystery.

Nestled into the mountains, alongside the lake, and insulated by the trees, the setting holds us collectively in the palm of her hand. Together, these gods conspire to nurture our souls. In this holding and this nurturing we are reminded that we are part of the nature we see, and as such we belong. We see in the beauty of nature, the beauty that lies in each of us, both within ourselves and in our physical bodies. We are part of this; we are of the earth. Emerald Lake reminds us of this. Moore writes "Spiritually, nature directs our attention toward eternity, but at the same time it contains us and creates an intimacy with our own personal lives that nurtures the soul" (Moore, 1996b, p. 5). A participant phrased it this way:

> Part of the physical isolation, beauty and inherent sacredness of Emerald Lake is an offering, to those who chose, to find the earth's voice and hence to touch their own soul. For all

participants, I believe, the physical surroundings enhanced awareness of the immensity and power of the land, so easily lost in the closed circles of everyday life. It is so remote, so beautiful, so close to the earth and its spirits or gods. One cannot be there and not be affected by the vastness of the earth. It brings together both the sense of isolation and how small we are in the large scheme of nature, and which I believe inspires a need to connect with each other, to share part of our lives at a very deep level because we may feel so insignificant alone. I found my sacred place at NEL, discovering that spiritual connection at Emerald Lake that has allowed me to re-connect to it in other times and places.

Although Moore suggests that we need to slow down to be moved by nature, this is not always the case. Sometimes in a session in which we are so busy and intent, and the discourse so serious, I gaze out the window and am arrested by the triteness of our work in comparison to what one beholds through the glass. In our rushing, I am frozen. I am reminded how small my work world is, and how immense the universe. Nature can remind us who we are, and who we are not, what we can achieve, and what we cannot. Yet, at one and the same moment she reminds us that we are merely, and most importantly, stewards of the earth and our professions, and the services and social responsibility we hold dear.

In summary, the environmental factors, physical setting, and seclusion were inspiring, spiritually moving, and a powerful means to reinforce the importance of leadership that honors the environment. Celebration, ceremony, and the sacred were similarly important to leadership and are considered next.

## Celebration, Ceremony, and the Sacred

Dirkx (1997) suggests that any learning through soul, including learning to lead, calls for a more central role of imagination and fantasy in our instructional methods and content. Stories, narratives, myths, tales, metaphor, and ritual capture aspects of the world not always readily accessible through many teaching approaches. NEL uses celebration, ceremony, and ritual that all attend to, and honor, soul.

Ritual and ceremony are important aspects of leadership and offer a moving and magical element to NEL. An early ritual is used in which participants and mentors are given a stone, invited to invest their baggage, barriers, or other impediments to learning or leading, into the stone, and to throw it away. Results from my research indicated that this was a useful and meaningful experience. One participant noted:

> I felt a sense of boundlessness that I was completely opened up where all my fears, feelings, and doubts were exposed to myself and others. This was like a healing, like being cleansed or set free of so much baggage. Afterwards I was in a state of euphoria (for lack of a better word). I felt something when we threw the stones away—I was ready to throw that stone and ready to move on.

Another activity that occurs midway though the five days is a Celebration Dinner. At this dinner, participants and mentors are invited to wear clothing or bring items that reflect an aspect of themselves or an achievement they have made of which they are proud. During dinner, each person shares with the whole group what it is they are celebrating about themselves. While this can be an intimidating and difficult activity, and one not often undertaken in one's life, the effect can be very soulful, as well as important to leadership development. It is a moment in the program that achieves interpersonal openness in a positive light (as compared to a negative light which might involve disclosing a failure or challenge). One participant noted: "The sense of group, which was particularly strong after the Celebration Dinner, was very evident. Our group in particular felt that we had developed a synthesis for dealing with problems presented to us quickly and effectively." Another wrote: "I was most moved by the Celebration Dinner. I learned about myself and others in the library community."

Celebration and honoring of self are important aspects to valuing who we are, which enriches soul and enables us to lead, or to live, with joy. Some cultures are premised upon this idea:

The Balinese have much to teach us about the (non) art of celebration. The making of splendid occasions occupies much of their time. If you ask a Balinese what he does, he will proudly answer, "I am a Baris dancer" or "I am a mask maker." If you persist and ask again, "No, I mean how do you get your rice?" he loses interest, his voice drops, he may turn away, deciding this is a pretty boring conversation. "Oh that," he will say. (Kent, 1997, p. 121)

Closely related to celebration of self is commitment to self and to others. A commitment circle activity invites participants to make a verbalized commitment to themselves, the profession, or to others of importance. Of this activity, a participant noted:

I learned how to make commitments to myself at NEL. I am a great maker of commitments to others (personally and professionally) and am bound by them to keep them and fulfill them. I realized at NEL that I never make commitments to myself and have undertaken to change that. NEL gave me the opportunity to take the time to discover how important I am to myself. I need to celebrate myself and the power that I have to control my positive destiny.

Opportunities such as these are soulful and important because they resonate at a deep personal level, which is closely related to how we perceive ourselves in the world and at work. The opportunity to explore aspects of this within a professional context, with others who had similar dreams and aspirations, was important. As this participant noted:

There are two moments that I frequently return to: the commitment circle and the healing circle. I guess I return to these because I am baffled by how strong my emotional reactions were to these ceremonial processes. All the more so for someone like myself who tends not to openly express feelings of emotion. Perhaps listening to everyone else share their own feelings and passions about life and librarianship began to resonate with my own. I began to recognize the same hopes and dreams: wanting to participate, make things change, to make

things happen. What we do (as librarians) is important to us. I
think that's what I was really responding to.

A final closing ceremony, based in part on aboriginal cultural
practice, occurs at the end of the Institute. The ceremony is
designed to give each person the opportunity to express thoughts
or feelings they have about elements of the Institute, themselves,
or their experiences that they would like to share. A final ritual
in which participants are given a gift and welcomed into the
profession by its leaders leaves those involved very moved and
feeling honored and respected. The respondents indicated that
this was one of the most memorable moments for them, and
moved them beyond all else—as one participant wrote: "The
final ceremony touched my soul. I appreciated the giving of
time, energy, memories, and symbolic gifts to the participants.
That was a time for each of us to feel special, individually and
collectively."

The ceremony honors each person, the community and the
natural environment. A mentor noted:

I came away from both with a new and deeper understanding of
the sacred. Sacredness has had enormous significance to me for
many years, but I was amazed at how broad and deep it
became—especially after hearing the female spiritual leader at
NEL. It broadened my notion of stewardship. Librarians in some
sense have the stewardship of the recorded memory of mankind
[sic]. I was much affected by the treatment of the relationship
between the human being and the earth, which does not belong
to us, either; we are stewards of a certain trust in relation to the
earth. This was a powerful connection for me.

Some also indicated that it was among the most spiritual life
moments they have known. For others, it was an opportunity to
recapture something lost, or to be reminded of the importance of
the sacred in their lives, as noted by this participant:

A moment I recall most was during the sweet-grass ceremony, a
spiritual experience. This is a rarity for me, to experience
anything that I would term spiritual. Once a Christian believer
who lost her faith, I guess I fight hard not to let that part of me

come alive. Maybe it's a protective gesture? That way I won't have to deal with the unsettledness that was so painful during the period when my faith failed me. In any case, the sweet-grass ceremony gave me the safety to experience this facet of myself again.

For others, such as this participant, the ceremony became very specifically tangible, in a spiritual way:

I had what you call a spiritual experience, an event that owed itself to many things. Such as changes that were taking place in my personal life, the magic and majesty of the mountains, the intensity of the sessions and certainly the appearance of Bruce Starlight. The religious closing ceremony had very special meaning for me because of my past involvement with shamanism and my own spiritual beliefs and needs at the time. However, I'm still not sure if such an event was appropriate for the group and believe that those who believe in the traditional church may very well have felt awkward about the entire event. I loved it and hope that I might one day see Bruce again. In terms of real impact I would say Bruce Starlight moved me at a spiritual level. Bruce really sent me over the top; it was a terrific experience. The power which came across in the pipe ceremony cannot be described appropriately. As they say, "you just know"—a silence that cannot be described but is spiritually uplifting. The intensity of the sessions and the group bond which developed all had something to do with the greatness of the event.

Although the ceremony was designed to honor each person, such expressions are not common in our experience, and may elicit feelings of unworthiness, as this participant shares: "Another memory is of the [gift] giving ceremony, and of my fellow group members' faces streaming with tears. (Mine was the same.) The beauty of the gesture was overpoweringly powerful. There was a feeling of unworthiness—I can't possibly be worthy of such a wonderful gift—coupled with a simultaneously occurring feeling of worthiness—yes, I am, and will be, worthy of this."

However, this person did decide that she was going to be worthy of such caring, attention, and gift. This is an important element of leadership as well: to accept such treatment and gifts, and to feel worthy of them. For some, the ceremony left people with an individual feeling of hope for themselves in the future, as this participant noted: "The closing service was great. Coming from a church-affiliated institution, I am very used to experiencing and sharing in moments of a spiritual nature. I remember the speaker talking of being true to oneself. I wish that I could say that I have learned from that. Does anyone really ever achieve this? Always good to have goals, I guess."

Ceremony, ritual, and attending to sacred aspects of our lives has, for many, become a rare event, and a great loss. As individuals, as leaders and as a society, we need these elements to provide a richness, depth, and sense of the sacred.

At NEL, an aboriginal sweet-grass and pipe ceremony was chosen because it is part of the aboriginal ancestry of the Director at NEL, Ernie Ingles. The ceremony has significance in Ernie's own history, and he believed that it would bring a rich and appreciated dimension to NEL. I was also curious about aboriginal sweet-grass ceremonies, and was comfortable with this choice as an activity, as were the other program planners.

The vast majority of respondents found this to be among the most profoundly moving experiences at NEL, and moved many at a deep soulful level. Some respondents felt privileged to experience another culture, as this respondent noted: "The sweet-grass and pipe ceremony was also profoundly moving on the level of having the opportunity to peek into, and at some level participate in, another group's ritual—one vested in a lot of significance and mystery. I felt privileged to be able to take part in it."

Another participant echoed the idea just presented, but added another dimension that illustrates that sharing of another culture sometimes allows us to learn more about ourselves and each other. In this case, the openness of this cultural ceremony helped this group to be more open themselves and to glimpse in others that which would otherwise be unseen. As one mentor expressed:

The opportunity to share a ritual from the original peoples of North America was profoundly moving. The two men were gracious in presenting to us, and I was reminded of other rituals I have been able to experience. I was acutely aware of our privileged window on something both ancient and, fortunately, still living. I was deeply affected by hearing the admissions of some of the men, in particular, of what previous NEL experiences had meant to them. Because there's a cluster of people in the group I have known for some time, I can observe personally what changes have occurred in them, but it was especially moving to hear change acknowledged by others. What a powerful event!

While some see it as a privilege and an opportunity to learn aspects of another culture, others see it as an unnecessary event or perhaps even an appropriation of an already exploited and marginalized group. This idea has been expressed through aboriginal criticism as well. For my part, as an educator, I am always interested in sharing with learners aspects of other cultures. Through activities such as these, leaders are able to reinforce their ability to have compassion and tolerance for diversity which respects others.

While striving to appreciate others, it is useful to remember that many aboriginal traditions are also part of the histories of many global cultures. Drumming, for example, has been ascribed to those of Mediterranean, Asian, and European ancestry (Redmond, 1997). The use of circles has been important as well, such as that discovered at Stonehenge, near Bath, England, and with the pyramids. It is good for the soul that we allow and attend to our collective history. As this participant comment illustrates, there are many similarities, as well as opportunities for sharing, between religious and cultural traditions: "As a Buddhist, I found this ceremony a very powerful and communal experience and an amazing sharing of our humanity, frailty and compassion."

Overall, the ceremonies that were part of NEL helped to solidify the community that the group work initiated. Like caring previously discussed, it seems ceremony allowed colleagues to join in community, as this participant noted: "We were touched at a deep level. The smoking of the pipe and the blankets are the most remembered ceremonial/ritual aspects for me. I remember feeling, for the first time to any significance, heartfelt feelings for people I had only allowed to be colleagues before."

Ceremony solidifies community, encourages exploration of personal spirituality, reminds us to honor self and others—all of which is deeply personal, soulful, and nurtures courage to lead.

## Impact of NEL on Career and Life: To Lead or Not to Lead

Respondents to my research were asked if they believed the experience of NEL had a lasting impact on their career. Over 62% of participants and 63% of mentors believed that NEL had a lasting impact on their careers. Over 33% of participants and 36% of mentors believed that NEL had a long lasting impact on their lives.

NEL had a lasting impact *on career* for over half of the participants, and *on life* for a third of participants. Fleming determined that "The residential dynamic seems to capture and envelop the whole learner, enabling her to bring all of herself to her learning, and to take away from that experience all that she is able to take" (p. 268). In her research, the impact was more short-term than long-term. As noted above, these findings are generally similar for the mentor group as well. It does seem that the combination achieved at NEL, as both a residential experience, and one that aligns seniors and juniors within a professional-based learning dynamic, does result in a lasting impact. However, the question regarding long-term impact merits further longitudinal study, given the relatively short time between each NEL and the time of my research.

One of the primary ways in which NEL impacted respondents on a long-term basis was through renewed interest in, and energy for, the profession. One participant characterized it this way: "Yes, the experience of NEL had a lasting impact on my career and life in general. It renewed my energy at the time, and renewed my interest in librarianship and learning. I still hope to someday be driven by a strong vision of my own, and to be able to help as many people as the NEL people have. I continue to work towards being part of a strong library community in my region."

For some, that energy was complemented by a more positive outlook, which resulted in an increased desire to assume leadership roles, as this person describes:

The Northern Exposure experience for me was life changing, career affirming and enlightening. The largest impact it left on me was to change the nature of my thinking—I learned the power of positive thinking and afterward I felt that I could do anything with my life or career if I wanted to. I suppose it gave me a sense of empowerment that profoundly changed me. I had always been a positive person who believed in myself but when I came to NEL I was starting to doubt everything, especially the choices I had made. I was having second thoughts about the choice I had made to go to library school, to become a librarian and then to take a job in the dreaded public library. NEL came just in the nick of time for me for I was starting to lose my interest in my work. After NEL I decided to remain a librarian and stay in my hometown public library because I know I can make a difference. It may sound strange, but I truly feel that my library needs me not only now in my work as a public service librarian, but in a future leadership position (which I am slowly working toward).

Some credit NEL for their decision to change jobs, or seek new positions, as this participant described: "Yes, NEL had a lasting impact on my career. Within a year of my return I was in a teaching position and had walked away from the "library" although I was teaching in a library tech program. Two years after that I assumed responsibility as the program head, the experience in that position landed me my new job as head of the [library department]."

Some felt that such encouragement, though, resulted in a feeling of obligation to contribute. This participant illustrates a struggle to manage the feeling of obligation:

NEL instilled in me a sense of obligation to participate actively in my organizational and professional life—not necessarily at all times, but at least from time to time. And because it is only two years since, the choices I made immediately following NEL are still in place—namely to take on positions of leadership in both my place of work and in my territorial library association, both of which bear two-year terms. NEL inspired me to take the risk of putting myself "out there." I have learned from this that this kind of role is not for me—whether or not I have done a good job (and one can never really know, I suppose), it is an unhappy one for me. My preferred role of participant but not leader is the one to which I will return. Such self-knowledge is valuable in one's quest for peace, and I would never have known without NEL because I would not have tried. I refer here to the formal kind of leadership—chairing committees, associations, etc.—not the qualities of leadership that anyone might exhibit at various times.

Although not everyone is comfortable with assuming leadership positions, the participant above reported trying to address that sense of obligation, and attaining greater self-understanding in the process. It is valuable to notice that although participants may feel a sense of obligation, they are managing that feeling in different ways, and report the ways in which they are working to find a comfortable balance. While some felt the need to accomplish much, others felt a release from feeling that they had to accomplish much, or be all things to all people: "At NEL I realized that what I do and what I had done up to that point was okay — that I was a good worker, that I was valued and respected among my colleagues, and I did have something to contribute. NEL helped me realize that I did not have to kill myself or stretch myself so thin that it was affecting my health."

Another participant made a similar assertion: "NEL impacted primarily on my career. Although still difficult, I am now more willing to stay where I am. I am less eager to move up the professional ladder as quickly as possible. There are other influences keeping me here, but the experience at NEL makes it easier to bear."

Although NEL is intended to enrich and develop leadership skills, and does encourage professional involvement, some of those who do not wish to pursue such activities, or find doing so difficult for any number of reasons, find support to avoid doing so. This support was in some cases attributed to NEL generally, but respondents did not identify specific aspects of NEL that assisted them in feeling content to maintain a level of involvement that suited them. However, one might surmise that they may feel more comfortable doing less because they feel accepted and validated in community with others.

For another, the feeling of connection was extended to a feeling of having faith in the profession by meeting those they would call leaders and mentors:

> I believe that the experience has had a great impact on my career. I went to NEL wondering how I was going to get out of libraries and move on to my next career. Librarianship is my second career and I was beginning to feel the need to move in a new direction and to be honest, I was hoping that it would be one that would take me out of libraries. I work in a very dysfunctional work environment and there are few here that I would or could envision as mentors. There has been poor leadership within our institution for quite some time and I had begun to feel rather hopeless about this environment ever becoming a positive opportunity for me. At NEL I had the chance to sit back and gain a new perspective on my current work environment, where I need to grow and go, and my future (either here or elsewhere). I gained insight that there may be a path out of this despair and it may be within myself. I am hopeful that even if no concrete opportunities for advancement come for me inside this workplace, I am a different person within myself and can survive and even lead from within. I believe that I will now be able to recognize it when the time comes to leave and move on.

The person above also alludes to the long-term impact of greater self-understanding, self-confidence, self-appreciation, as this participant also noted:

I shed a lot of tears at NEL—it was like a cleansing was taking place. Along with this cleansing feeling I was also crying because I was a bit fearful of the challenges that lay ahead. I now had to face the world with this new resolve and with a vision. At work I had to learn to stand up for myself and not feel that I constantly had to prove myself. In my personal life I was truly on my own. I shed the obsession that I had with trying to make somebody love me that could not love me for me. I gained self-acceptance and self-confidence at NEL.

For some, NEL helped them to recognize the challenges that they saw for themselves in their futures. For others, NEL was a reminder to recognize the challenges they had met, to give themselves credit for that, and to remember to look at the bigger picture in order to see that more clearly:

I did have an experience at NEL that could be described as an emotional, spiritual, or soulful one. I will do my best to describe it: The weather tended to be overcast and drizzly when I was at NEL. As a result, the path up to the lodge was often wet and slippery so I was always looking down to make sure that I wouldn't have any unpleasant surprises. One morning, on my way up the path to breakfast, I paused and looked upwards. The path seemed to go up and beyond the lodge and lead directly to a snow-topped mountain. A ray of sunlight had just burst through the clouds and had transformed the snow into sparkling diamonds. Of course I knew that there were mountains all round, but I had been so busy concentrating on not slipping, I had forgotten that they were there. I realized then that this experience could be applied to my view of life. I do have a tendency to get so concerned about the details and the negative aspects of a situation that I can miss the satisfaction or the thrill of knowing that I really have made a contribution or accomplished something significant. I later took a photograph of the path and the mountain to remind me of this moment. I have 8-by-11 inch enlargements of the photograph on my desk at work and on my dresser at home. The picture certainly doesn't come anywhere near to replicating the splendor of the mountain, but it is enough to keep my memory alive.

On the other end of the continuum, some mentors reported being pleased to give something back, at this point in their career:

> Certainly it has had a lasting impact on my career. I just do business differently, inside and out! Specifically, there's a group of people out there for who I have a continuing responsibility. I seek them out when I can, and I listen to them. Many of them, in turn, keep my candles lit, and mentor me in their way. It surprises them when I say that, but I know it to be a common experience among mentors. NEL had a strong role in the integration of my professional and personal life, which were never terribly far apart in the first place. But the integration is more comfortable, a better fit.

Even mentors who were nearing the end of their career, NEL had a long-term impact on their work. One mentor stated: "On my career: in one sense, little, since I am at the end of the 'go-to-business-daily' phase. However, the sharper understanding I have of my emotional nature will contribute to the writing and free-lancing that I will continue to do. So, in the broad sense, there will be considerable impact."

While the foregoing section on career impact also addresses in some measure life impact, a number of respondents also reported specific life changes. For one participant, long-term impact was achieved through greater insight about and understanding of family members: "One moment I recall was during the workshop on change when I realized my family/spouse was not going to change the way I had hoped, that they wanted to stay in Egypt, as it were. This was a shocking realization—no, not a realization because I had always known this deep down. No, at that moment I was forced to accept a truth I didn't want to admit."

The next participant claimed to have greater self-understanding and reported long-term family benefits: "I believe that my personal life has benefited from this experience. The spill-over from my happy home-life will be beneficial to my work-life."

The search for long-term effects continues for some. Although believing that NEL was significant, this participant, like others, reported an ongoing search for ways to incorporate the experience into life in a way that will make a difference:

> I find this to be a very searching question, which frequently plagues me. I found NEL to be an extremely significant experience, which I judge should have had a significant impact on my career. The problem is, it has made no discernible difference. I see this as totally my own lack, not a deficiency of NEL. I keep remembering different lessons about being a leader, making a difference, etc.—and thinking that I ought to be able to implement some of that in my work life now. But the fact is, I haven't been able to. I only hope that eventually I will.

NEL had a long-term effect on participants that affect both life and career, with a concentration on the latter. Career effects include a feeling of renewed energy and commitment to the profession, and a greater feeling of being part of a larger community. On personal and individual levels, respondents reported greater understanding, acceptance, and appreciation of self as well as family members. For mentors, the opportunity to give something back to the profession was primary.

## The Harvest

NEL inspires leadership and nurtures soul through: attention to the importance of relationships within a professional caring community with peers, mentors and self; ceremony, symbol, and the sacred; risk; struggle and disclosure; ethics; creativity and imagination; physical environment; and residential factors such as shared accommodations and meals. These, in addition to the use of a variety of teaching methods, with a particular concentration on experiential learning, resulted in a long-term impact. More to the point, the confluence of these moved over 93 percent of respondents at a soul level. For many, NEL profoundly moved them, taught them in a unique way, and quite simply, made magic.

The element most strongly commented upon in learning to lead was the human relationships that were formed between peers and mentors, as well as the increased understanding, appreciation for, and acceptance of self. Participants and mentors alike noted the importance of the personal and professional relationships, as well as the friendships and networks that were formed. Working in consistent groups was important to that process, and those involved felt like they were part of a caring community. There were many noted who were moved by the caring of mentors, which enabled participants to feel affirmed and appreciated. They felt they were connected through the experience, and that they now had a "human face" and recognized as simply people, those who were otherwise a group of remote, unknown, larger-than-life leaders. Participants particularly appreciated that such "high profile" leaders would take time and invest energy in creating and sustaining such a rich opportunity for young professionals. Group work with mentors as well as the personal storytelling that the mentors provided were augmented by informal socializing and shared meals. The nature of the mentoring was educational and professional, and occurred on a person-to-person basis, as well as a group-to-group basis—as senior to junior professionals. Taken together, the diversity of the mentoring was affirming, informative, and relayed feelings of community and caring. This participant addresses the human factor, and hints at career-related issues:

There was the realization that we are all human and all essentially made of the same substance. That we all have the same potential for fear, happiness, joy, courage, desperation, and so many other senses and emotions. It is what we do with these that will be the mark of our success, not the weakness of having had the fear or experiencing the desperation. The realization of all of this was a great source of strength to me—to see such great leaders who have had (and continue to have—damn those boomers!) such great careers also be human was a revelation. I don't have many wonderful mentors around me here in ****, but I now have many in my fellow participants and mentors from NEL.

The work-related issues are complex, and positive and negative. As well as being moved at a soulful level at NEL, the majority of respondents noted that it did have a long-term effect on their careers or their lives. This was found in a renewal of energy and interest, sense of community within the profession, and feeling affirmed as a professional. Some respondents noted seeking out leadership positions, getting more involved with professional activities, and generally feeling that they could achieve anything they wanted to. Many mentors felt re-energized in their work, and satisfied in the knowledge that they had "given something back" to their profession. They too, in turn, commented upon the hope that the participants inspired, and upon the faith they had that the future of the profession was in good hands.

As a professional adult education experience, NEL is closely related to the workplace, as well as the professional community. It is evident that people invest much in their work and professions and care about them deeply. A sense of identity emanates from work, and to be respected within that role as a professional moves people at a very deep and soulful level. As this participant noted: "The discussions touched my vocation about which I am passionate and can be moved to tears. My choice of profession has much to do, for me at least, with living my values, with the heart of my soul."

However, as noted by a couple of respondents to my research of the previous chapter, that when respect and affirmation are not found upon return to the workplace, dissonance results that can be painful to the soul. Some respondents noted that the absence of any changes in their work position left them feeling "plagued" with questions about why they were not advancing, or frustrated and disheartened that they were not.

There is a need, identified both in this research as well as in the literature, to incorporate aspects of soul into the workplace. Yet, it would be unfortunate if employers sought to appropriate soul as a means to extract more labor from the labor force. It would be regrettable if soul became the latest iteration of the work ethic under the spirit of capitalism, as the total quality management framework has been criticized for doing. It can be envisioned that corporate opportunists may seek to exploit this dimension of human existence. Yet, some respondents alluded to the lack of soul in the workplace, and resulting feelings of alienation. In terms of work, a balance between incorporating soul, while not exploiting it, is important. Writers such as Dirkx (1996) and Briskin (1996) address the need to incorporate aspects of soul within the workplace as well.

Another important aspect relating to human relationships concerns the relationship with self. Participants felt greater self-respect, self-understanding, and self-acceptance. One participant noted being moved that she now knew that "it was possible to live a vision of an expanded self." A number of participants noted that subsequent to NEL, they had a greater awareness of their own needs and preferences, as well as a greater ability to negotiate the difficulties they faced within their relationships at work and at home. Through self-understanding, some noted that now they were more comfortable with remaining in their current job situation and not aspiring to greater hierarchical positions, such as this participant noted: "After the retreat, the most profound effect on me spiritually was that I have wanted to remove myself from the very things that I think NEL promotes—ambition, inspiring others, rising to new heights in career, etc."

People were both affirmed as individuals and as members of a group. Rather than feeling alienated in a profession or as a human being, people felt connected and an important and integral part of their profession through the NEL experience. Perhaps affirmation in their role and place in the world, rather than their cognitive view of the world, as well as the connection with mentors and peers, resulted in feelings which impact at a soulful level. People came to care for and respect each other. As one participant said: "There are some very sad moments where people are sharing incredibly personal things and you feel like this is part of your own family. Not that its happening to you, but you feel this incredible compassion for what people have gone through. And you realize the real lows that come in life and the importance of having support around you."

There are a number of elements to consider which augment relationships with self and others. The symbolic events at NEL were also very important. The ceremonial, ritualistic, and celebratory events were often noted as a means to connect with and appreciate inner dimensions of self. This element was also noted in relation to feeling connected with a broader community. The investing of baggage into a stone and tossing it away was a ritualistic physical means through which respondents became open to learning and to leadership. The celebration dinner midway through the Institute was an opportunity for greater group bonding, both within the small workgroups as well as with the larger group. And the final series of rituals, including the commitment circle, the sweet-grass ceremony and the gifting ceremony solidified the community feeling, enabled participants to feel authentically valued by library leaders, and even allowed and permitted a cathartic moment of tears, which many noted would normally be avoided.

Another aspect that was important in the experience was the physical environment. NEL was held in a secluded place of natural stillness and beauty. As one participant put it, "I knew something magical would happen" the moment she arrived on site, with the surrounding mountains to serve as "stairs from the valley and steps to the sun's retreats" (Birney, 1959, p. 347). The natural environment was considered central to the experience of eliciting soul, and inspiring leadership, as was the opulent accommodations and luscious meals.

Part of the impact that NEL has can be attributed to the environment itself, but also to what the environment means in the lives of some, if not many of the participants. As average income earners, many young librarians would not have much opportunity to enjoy an experience such as this. As one participant wrote: "I was touched by the wonderful way that I was treated by the Institute. I have spent so long as a student and as the director of a poor library, that I have come to feel that doing things on the cheap is normal, and perhaps all that librarians deserve. It was a delight, then, to be treated with such opulence, and such attention to detail."

In closing, leadership education forums such as Northern Exposure to Leadership, and Snowbird are having an important impact on library leadership in North America. It certainly is touching the lives of many. As noted by this person: "There is a magic at NEL that is felt by most of the participants and many of the mentors and others. If one is prepared to allow it, the magic insinuates itself under one's professional and emotional facade to enrich and relieve many facets of our lives." This writing has become, ultimately, a rendering of that magic, and itself a celebration of it.

# Chapter Five

# And What of You and Me:
# Leading with Soul in the Workplace

Almost by definition, the workplace is structured to enhance corporate interests at the expense of both individuals and the community. In such an environment, individuals suffer when they and their labor are viewed as means to an end. Goals are predefined to enhance the bottom line, and processes are structured and predetermined. Attempts to build work teams, and movements such as Total Quality Management are critiqued as being a means to extract more labor from the labor force.

The current work situation of mechanized labor has been traced historically by Briskin (1996) who formulates linkages to the decline of soul in the workplace. Briskin, in *The Stirring of Soul in the Workplace,* explores the demise of soul in human labor during the rise of capitalism, which suppresses soul at work in order to create a more compliant labor force. He traces the means of this through the use of the panopticon in which workers can be viewed at their jobs, to timeclocks and Taylorism on through to modern technology and automated systems which track labor productivity. Briskin describes the panopticon as a development of Bentham (1791) who realized that power would become contingent upon the ability to control human minds, bodies, and functionality. Bentham wanted to build an architectural structure that would enable constant scrutiny of those within it. School children, workers, convicts, and patients could all be secluded and observed at a distance, so that an overseer could view every aspect of behavior and movement to achieve desirable behavior and order, and maintain a system of hierarchy, classification, and surveillance. The panopticon for labor was developed during a time of changing economic conditions, when the newly industrializing areas needed a large labor pool and thus could be "a mill for grinding rogues honest and idle men industrious." Complementing this, Taylorism emanates from the thinking and work of Frederick

Taylor (1856-1915) who feverishly sought efficiency, precision mechanization, and management in the workplace. Much of the dehumanizing nature of work is traced to his tenets, the legacy of which is a workplace with little human value, collective purpose or individual meaning (Briskin, 1996). With the contributions of Bentham and Taylor, once human bodies were controlled, souls were then more easily suppressed.

Briskin supplements his analysis with an exploration of the perpetuation of the cult of efficiency and the work ethic, in which "the underlying rules that govern the system—where power is actually located—are invisible. Domination is not simply a function of one thing, whether surveillance, architecture or punishment; it is an elemental force that feels pervasive. Everyone feels watched and judged" (p. 81). And all are caught. The watchers are watched too, and feel the pressure and scrutiny to lesser and greater degrees from peers and colleagues within professional contexts.

In these contexts, people may be changed from the inside out, wherein individuals are required to tame their own human nature. When people police themselves for the benefit of approval and capital, their very souls are at risk. They may come to wonder who they are, ponder the authentic nature and needs of their souls, and question whether or not they truly have one. Two sociologists tried to capture elements of this: Emile Durkheim called this *anomie*, and Karl Marx called it *alienation*. In my estimation, when there is a sense of detachment in relation to our labor it may be because human souls are transmogrified by capital. Thus, it could be said that as people sell their labor, they sell their souls. If they indeed, inherently, put their souls on the auction block along with their labor, they are, in essence, selling their souls. Hades cannot be far behind. How can this be avoided? Briskin (1996) offers some suggestions in his discussion about soul within the context of the organizational group:

> Organizations are places where what is unique about the individual meets what is unique about social organization. Increasingly, organizations are where we spend the majority of our time and where the stirrings of the soul are often perceived

as absent. To explore the challenge to the human soul in organizations is to build a bridge between the world of the personal, subjective, and even unconscious elements of individual experience and the world of organizations that demand rationality, efficiency, and personal sacrifice. For the individual, there is often no clear distinction between these worlds. We are both individuals and member of groups within organizations. We cannot leave behind who we are when we are inside organizations any more than we can shut out the organization when we are alone. We carry inside us all the time both the organization in our mind and the person we think we are. When there is a fit, we sense harmony and balance. When these two worlds collide, however, the individual feels torn and alone. (p. xvi)

This is true in most organizations, and is particularly observable in organizations that are built upon the uniqueness of individuals and premised upon not only supporting, but requiring that people do that which they love. People in many professions expect that those who choose to do particular types of work choose those professions because they are called to that type of work. This is also the case within some institutions, such as universities. Faculty, for example, are expected to not only teach and research in their chosen fields, but are implicitly expected to care profoundly and passionately about what they do. Fortunately, as interests may shift throughout a career, faculty members are able to shift the focus of their work. There are additional complexities in some institutions that have a built in religious or spiritual code, such as the academy where I work. As a Catholic person (of sorts) in a Catholic institution that doesn't require its members to be Catholic, I have nonetheless found myself questioning my administrative decisions wondering how they fit within a Catholic, Christian, caring, and self-sacrificing community. For example, if a request I make is good for the library, and a reasonable request, I may still question: Am I being selfish? Am I asking for too much? What are my intentions? For whom, truly, am I asking? What will be thought of my request? In these cases, the call to work, and to do my job, involves questions of self-reflection, as it would for anyone, but somehow the need for reflection feels more compelling because of the nature of the institution itself. As expressed by Briskin "so often in organizations we are trying to figure out the motives of others, assess our job functions, address the expectations of bosses, subordinates, and peers. We lose ourselves, our own images, of what organizations mean to us" (Briskin, 1996, p. 211). In cases such as these, otherwise common workplace issues and decisions get caught in a dynamic with elements that are spiritual and soulful, and teasing out one from the other is not easily achieved. Yet, while this struggle exists, I am eternally grateful that it does, for it enables me to bring all of my humanity to my work, to ask myself who I am and who I want to become. Because my College is premised upon Catholic social teaching and human justice, I can be kind and compassionate with my staff, my colleagues and myself. On the days I need to, I can be a mom first, and leave work when I have to. Similarly, because it is an academic institution, I can spend time doing research and writing, and write in the style I prefer, which is beyond dry, academic discourse. If we are lucky and blessed, our work can draw us into our humanity, in various ways, as much as it draws us away from our humanity.

Briskin's earlier description of the demise of soul in the workplace and my situation at work are two sides of the same coin. In the former, the world is too much with us, and sometimes in the latter, the soul is too much with us. The tensions must be navigated as we each seek to either inject elements of soul into the workplace, or set boundaries around ourselves in terms of what can and cannot be required of us. For each of us, when all is said and done, as Briskin (p. 87) reminds us:

> You cannot be someone else. You cannot gain freedom by conforming. You cannot adapt yourself to circumstances and then feel you are a victim or a bystander. I recall a story from my own childhood about a certain Rabbi Zusya, who said, "In the coming world they will not ask me: Why were you not Moses or Akiba or Abraham? They will ask me: Why were you not Zusya?"

This reminds me of an encounter I had with an elderly woman in Medicine Hat. A couple of colleagues, Ernie Ingles and Dr. Merrill Distad, and I had gone to visit a donor after meetings in Calgary, Alberta. The three of us had gone to the local fair the evening before our meeting with the woman, let our hearts rise and fall on the Ferris Wheel, eaten cotton candy, and behaved as much like children as the three of us could manage—they being highly sophisticated and well educated, and I being young and naively trying to impress. I commented about our evening to the woman the following day. She looked me squarely in the eye and said, with the wisdom of the teacher she was: "You know my dear, you can only fake it for so long at work, and then people are bound to find out who you really are."

In our work, as in our lives, the past of who we were, the present of who we are, and the future of who we dream to become merge together along with the inside and the outside of the three, much like the prisms of a kaleidoscope: converging and diverging, reflecting and refracting, spilling and casting color. Theologian Matthew Fox writes that work "comes from the inside out; work is the expression of our soul, our inner being. It is unique to the individual; it is creative. Work is an expression of the Spirit at work in the world through us. Work is that which puts us in touch with others, not so much at the level of personal interaction, but at the level of service in the community" (Fox, 1994, p. 5).

There are creative ways in which soul can be stirred into the workplace, the expanse of which is limited only by the expanse of our imaginations. We can do this for ourselves as well as for those whom we supervise. For my part, I have considered what I can do in terms of responsibilities, required and voluntary, environment, policies, practices, relationships and opportunities for creativity. I welcome responsibilities that align with my idea of valuable work. I ask: is this a task that has purpose and meaning to myself or others? In my volunteer work, I hope to enrich the lives of others, at activities that range from a leadership institute for librarians, to listening to grade two students reading aloud. Environmentally, in my office and in my library, I've created a space that incorporates warm colors, art from the campus Kenderdine Collection, and plants. I indulge my desire to create by periodically designing displays suitable to current events, or highlighting parts of the library's collection, such a recent showing of our illuminated manuscripts. I create policies and procedures that are consistent with my own ideas of justice and fairness, and I am likely to err on the side of compassion and leniency than rigor and strictness.

I try to incorporate aspects of compassion and caring in my work relationships as well. Sometimes easier said than done, I've had the experience of asking my supervisor to remember that I, as a whole person, come in to work each day, and they get all of me: my hopes, dreams, desires, and problems, my passion and creativity as well as less favorable attributes such as my pride in my need for recognition and respect. It can be the case too that these things are amorphous and uncertain, but my soul knows when it is longing, or when it has been assaulted by what I might characterize as subtle and sophisticated workplace slights or bullying. A colleague of mine, for example, relays how in her organization, she is not greeted by another in the hall as they are passing, or acknowledged by another in meetings. In organizations where greeting another is common and expected, withholding a greeting can feel ostracizing.

On the other hand, we can take advantage of opportunities to honor and care for each other in the workplace. A staff member of mine recently relayed to me her appreciation that I not only care *for her*, but also take care *of her* in ways that are welcome and soulful. When she was having trouble with her eyes, I acquired new task lighting for her desk, and a new, clear computer monitor. When she appears tired in the mid to late afternoon, I might suggest she go home early and have a cup of tea. When she was struggling with a personal issue, I purchased an inexpensive Chagal umbrella, and gave her a card that read: *When life rains on your parade, sometimes the best we can do is to carry a beautiful umbrella.* These small efforts resulted, she suspected, in a pain leaving her neck that had been there for some years. Reciprocally, she takes care of me by managing the circulation desk and its staff, serving as a sounding board for my administrative frustrations, helping me to understand corporate culture and history, bringing me homemade chutneys and baking, counseling me about raising my son (she has four grown children) and suggesting books I might like to read from our own collection, which are new to me and very well known by her. This related thought of Mother Teresa comes from one of them: "The biggest disease today is not leprosy or tuberculosis, but rather the feeling of being unwanted, uncared for and deserted by everybody. The greatest evil is the lack of love and charity, the terrible indifference towards one's neighbor" (Muggeridge, 1971, p. 73). Although Mother Teresa worked in the streets of Calcutta, a very poor place, she also worked in the city of London. Her assertion in this case can apply to any environments in which humans live and interact, including the workplace.

For my part, bringing soul to the workplace has been made possible through my research and writing this book. It has indeed been a great gift to regard the soul, and to explore it as a topic such as this one tantamount to our very existence:

> When Socrates addressed the senators of Athens at his trial he didn't ask for their mercy or forgiveness or even defend himself. Instead, he asked why they weren't ashamed of spending their lives hoarding money and fame and *"caring so little about wisdom and truth and the greatest improvement of the soul, which you never regard at all."* (Cousineau, 1994, p. 120)

The opportunity to undertake research of this nature, and to engage in discourse of this sort is a privilege for so many reasons, not least among them is the self-growth that one experiences in doing so. This topic, in particular, has been delightfully moving and fulfilling; it has enhanced my ability to attend to my own soul, enriched its dimensions, and informed my attempt to honor the soul of others. For this, I am grateful. While not always easy, it was an informative process. I am a different sort of librarian, leader, follower, and teacher as a result of this work. I now consider the importance of soul, and understand more fully its place within leadership, work, and education contexts.

Leaders and followers seek to know and understand who they are. As a metaphor, and literally, my research and writing has enabled me to do that. Sue Scott (1997) suggests that soul work is transformative and that is not easy. It is hard and makes one vulnerable. She notes that often people go into a kind of hibernation, work on art projects, or use their hands in some way. In development of the brain, the body is often regarded as an appendage or house, while a reintegration of the body and mind is soul work. Doing my doctoral research enabled me to paint, an ability I didn't know I had, and painting has enabled me to see myself and the world differently. It has allowed me to see color. Where I once saw only greens and blues and reds, I now see hues of ochre and lavender and chartreuse and crimson and pumpkin. Painting was a powerful teacher for me and was crucial during this process. It offered a channel into my soul and a conduit to allow elements of my soul to be released. Painting provided animation of the idea that each of us is unique and sees the world uniquely. Upon that seeing, we each then render it in our own hand. Art, in its doing and its viewing, has a unique capacity to awaken the soul, and teach it, like little else.

Personally, I often make choices employing cognitive forces, which are sometimes in direct opposition to intuitive and heartfelt choices. Undertaking this work has reinforced for me the inherent value of honoring intuitive and soulful aspects of myself. It has afforded me both the permission and the reason to read the types of literature that have been only at the margins of my life. Now, this seems so central to who I am and who I am becoming. Reading *When the Drummers Were Women*, an historical account dating to the sixth century B.C. of women drummers and goddesses, allowed me to gain an historical appreciation, to compliment a sociological interpretation, of the oppression and silencing of women. Recent interpretations such as those of Gilligan (1982) and Belenky, et al. (1986, 1997) coupled with my doctoral advisor's encouragement to let my voice be heard, gave me voice. Such reading also allowed an interpretive methodology that is closer to my own view of an expanding world beyond that of positivistic interpretations.

I have developed a further appreciation of aspects of soul, including the importance of place. I found it useful to undertake this research in a place that nurtured soul. I wrote part of this book in the Right Honourable John G. Diefenbaker Canada Centre, at the University of Saskatchewan, which overlooks the beautiful South Saskatchewan River valley. While there, I worked in what was the Director's windowless office, where I painted the beige walls salmon. There is no place to look out there, no window, so I had to look within—which, I think now, in retrospect, has served me well. I was immediately surrounded by some of Diefenbaker's books: his *Oxford English Dictionary* in 13 volumes; his collection of *Empire Club Address*; the *Masters of Eloquence* series (I should be so lucky); a 23-volume set from 1913 of *Canada and Its Provinces;* and *The Makers of Canada* in 21 volumes. I also had a collection of aboriginal, carved walking sticks and buffalo markers, as well as other art, which I acquired to support local artists. Finally, I had a two-foot high quartz sculpture of a squatting woman, elbows on knees with head in hands. She became my muse, and is the epitome of all I strive for: to live with grace and to remain humble. I have been blessed.

Another part of this book was written at my cottage at Sturgeon Lake in Northern Saskatchewan, which is a pristine fresh water lake with a river feeding and delivering it, teeming with pickerel and perch. I sit at the kitchen table, beside a McClary Royal Charm white cast-iron farm stove, which warms me as summer turns to fall. Pondering, I gaze across the morning deck, past the potted herb garden—rosemary, thyme, dill, parsley, lemon basil, and sage (which I burn in ritual), past the wide and soft, red Mexican hammock, past the squirrels who scamper hither and yon and compete for the nuts and seeds with the birds at the feeder, past the patio lanterns and Christmas lights that entwine the railing, past my son's hockey net, through the birch tree with leaves that jig in the wind, across and past and through all of this, to the lake. It is the lake itself that draws me here. Moving in one direction one day, and in the other the next, in seeming harmony with the prehistoric pelicans that fly to the west end of the lake in the morning and the east end in the evening. I wonder at it all. The name of the lake itself: Sturgeon, after a fish dating to prehistory, and the deep dark waters, with so much unseen and so much unknown. And ponder how it is that I have found my way to this place to write, and purchased this particular cottage to write about the people, the men and women, some of generations past, who have given so much to preserve and make present the written record of our world. They who have found a way of weaving the traditions of the past and of prehistory, into the present to create a form that is there and solid, but is fluid too, and sways gently in the breeze, allowing for movement, and holding the dreamer so that we, too, might gaze up to the heavens and imagine what we will.

This research and writing has enabled me to pause in an otherwise hectic life and consider a great question.

> By cultivating the ability of living in uncertainty without despair or surrender, we can respond to the godless hours and spiritless days with soulful moves from the garret and pulpit back to the street to answer the ground level question, *How should I actually live my life?* (Cousineau, 1994, p. 120)

The ways in which we are able to honor each other and inject soul into our work is limited only by the limits of our imaginations. I am confident that in your own work and at your own workplaces, you will also recognize ways in which you can be kind to—and take care of—yourself and others.

Efforts to take care of self and others are consistent with aspects of soul both inside and outside of the workplace, which as described by Elkins, makes place for the highs as well as the lows, for joy as well as sorrow. Work can be exciting and creative and allow for autonomy, or it can be repetitive and mindless and demand conformity. The tensions between the dichotomous poles must be massaged and balanced as we are each able to do in the creative ways we design to fit the specific nature of our individual workplaces. We must do this. We need to work, for our own individual expression and discovery of self, and also at a pragmatic level because we need to feed our children and ourselves.

Briskin suggests ways in which soul can be "stirred" into the workplace. One way in which this can be done is through self-examination with the objective of recognizing our own dark side. It is easy to know that of the other; management knows that of staff, and staff know that of management. But to recognize our own dark side, take responsibility for it, and work to change it is what will lead to organizational healing. While these are soulful approaches leading from the middle, there are also tips on pragmatic approaches worth noting.

Roger Fisher and Alan Sharp have written an excellent book entitled *Getting It Done: How to Lead When You're Not in Charge* (1998). This book offers a pragmatic tools and techniques approach to lateral leadership for those who are not in formal leadership positions, or are middle managers. Indeed, it is for anyone who realizes that they cannot accomplish their goals alone. They offer many tips on collaboration, personal skill development, purpose identification, collaborative vision creation and taking action. To begin, they suggest that we: 1) Ask questions that get others thinking about a situation and ask them for their thoughts in looking for a solution; 2) Offer your own thoughts, and invite others to use them, build upon them, or correct them; and 3) Do something that will serve as a model for better performance. They also explore what they identify as important leadership skills and offer ways in which those can be improved.

Similarly, Nancy Huber has written an excellent book called *Leading from Within: Developing Personal Direction* (1998). This book is without parallel in its presentation of tools, techniques, learning activities, and reflective questions to assist anyone undertaking leadership development. Huber is a leadership educator at the University of Arizona, and offers a personal, practical, and applied process to learning about leadership. This book provides a framework for exploring the reader's own ideas and philosophy about leadership, and exercises in clarifying personal vision and drafting personal mission statements. While learning to lead we each need to recognize a situation that needs attention and examine what is required to achieve a solution, create a plan to meet our desired ends, and then take action.

Robert Kelly has written an uncommon approach to the leadership literature that focuses on followers: *The Power of Followership: How to Create Leaders People Want to Follow and Followers Who Lead Themselves.* Kelly defines followers as people who know what to do (without being told) and act with intelligence, independence courage, and a strong sense of ethics. Kelly asserts that leadership is a myth, or a spotlight on select persons, and much of organizational success is achieved somewhere in the shadows. He critiques the lists that many leadership books present as requisite to lead, and suggests that few, if any, individuals have all or even many of the characteristics noted by any one of a number of authors. All leaders have some characteristics that are praiseworthy and others that are far from being so. All leaders are human, and we all have the capacity to lead. We all also have the capacity to follow, and Kelly suggests that the majority of us do so for about 70 to 90 percent of our working days. If this is true, how we follow is as important as how we lead, and organizations will fail without followers. His research indicates that followers at their best participate with enthusiasm, intelligence, and self-reliance, but without star billing. They focus on the goal, do a great job on critical activities, take initiative to add value to the organization, realize they add value in being who they are, and are team players. I would add that followers are also able to follow with a measure of trust that is premised upon the understanding that most leaders share our values, generally speaking, and that they are doing the best job they can. People in leadership positions typically have a broader view of the landscape: they interact with more people or stakeholders, hear more about different aspects of a situation, and are able to consider more information in decision making. Followers can exhibit grace and understanding by acknowledging this and giving leaders the benefit of the doubt. If one does need to take a stand, Kelly offers and describes ten steps you might follow: Be proactive, gather your facts, seek wise counsel before taking a stand, build your fortitude, work within the system, frame your position so that it will be heard, educate others on how your view serves their best interests, take collective action, seek higher authority if you meet leader resistance, and have the financial and emotional cushions to exercise other alternatives. As many of us know from experience or history, there are some leaders not to follow. Based on Kelly's surveys, he found that 2 out of 5 bosses have questionable abilities to lead, only one in seven is seen by others as someone to emulate, less than half of leaders are able to instill trust in subordinates, and nearly 40 percent have ego problems. If this is the norm, all organizational members have to form partnerships, and work together for organizational success.

# Conclusion

Leadership in librarianship has been premised upon great caring and passion embracing the soul's desire to do our best work while helping others. It is crucial that professions in the Western world begin to seriously explore aspects of the soul in all dimensions of life, including work. Or, perhaps if we do not, as Moore (1996a) suggests, ours will be a dangerous time. This will be because human community and civility are not humanistic achievements; they are the work of the ghosts of memory and the spirits of place, of the genius in things, and the soul of culture.

Attending to the soul in leadership is primary. I agree with Warren Bennis who asserts: "The point is not to become a leader. The point is to become yourself, to use yourself completely—all your skills, gifts, and energies—in order to make your vision manifest. You must withhold nothing. You must, in sum, become the person you started out to be, and enjoy the process of becoming" (1989, pp. 111-112).

As we become ourselves, we may reflect upon what has inspired us in our work lives, and continue our journey to create ourselves and ask ourselves two questions: When does one begin, given the incessant demands on our time and energy? We are often faced with daily demands that fritter away our lives;

we are faced with the dilemma of Michelangelo in Irving Stone's *The Agony and the Ecstasy* when asked to accept a commission that would have left him drained and uninspired, yet well paid, and was counseled by others to accept the commission. Thinking it would be fine to do so over the short run, he was admonished by the Prior Bichiellini: "'There are no long or short runs,' the prior cried, his voice heavy with indignation. 'There is only a God-given number of years in which to work and fulfill yourself. Don't squander them'" (1961, p. 368). And so Michelangelo created a rendering of David as he saw him; unlike the other artists before him who depicted a little man, with a fragile life seeking a home in eternity, he created a David that was a glorious creation of beauty, strength, courage, wisdom, and faith. His David would become Apollo, Hercules, and Adam. We must each consider that which is to be our David, so that we do not squander our precious time.

A second question is: How does one know which opportunities to pursue and which to let pass? We might ask ourselves, what causes me to lie awake at night? What causes me to laugh with joy or to weep with sorrow? We might seek to find, as suggested by Frederick Buechner (1973), the meeting place between the "world's deep hunger" and our own "deep gladness" and invite that intersection to be our point of departure, knowing as we do so that in the universe all things are possible, and that we create and recreate our world each and every day, with each and every decision. We must trust that the Universe holds all that we need, and believe that its abundance is available to us and intended for us to use in honorable and respectful ways, while being compassionate with those around us. May we do this with grace and courage and faith in the leadership of the Devine, holding sacred the knowledge that the Devine is in all things.

Then, may we know joy.

# References

Baldwin, Christina. (1998). *Calling the circle: The first and future culture.* New York: Bantam Books.

Barrett, William. (1986). *Death of the soul: From Descartes to the computer.* Garden City, N.Y.: Anchor Press/Doubleday.

Belenky, Mary Field, Blythe McVicker Clinchy, Nancy Rule Goldberger, and Jill Tarule Mattuck. (1986, 1997). *Women's ways of knowing: The development of self, voice and mind.* New York: Basic Books.

Bender, Peter Urs. (1997). *Leadership from within.* Toronto, Ontario: Stoddart Publishing.

Bennis, Warren. (1989). *On becoming a leader.* Reading, Mass.: Addison-Wesley.

Bennis, Warren. (1997). *Managing people is like herding cats.* Provo, Utah: Executive Excellence Publishing.

Berger, Peter, and Thomas Luckman. (1980). *The social construction of reality: A treatise in the sociology of knowledge.* New York: Irvington.

Birney, Earle. (n.d.) "David." In *A book of good poems* (1959). C. T. Fyfe. Toronto, Ontario: Copp Clark.

Block, Peter. (1993). *Stewardship: Choosing service over self-interest.* San Francisco, Calif.:Berrett-Koehler.

Briskin, Alan. (1996). *The stirring of soul in the workplace.* San Francisco: Jossey-Bass.

Brockmeyer-Klebaum, Donna. (2000). *Education to nurture the soul: An interpretive study of a leadership institute for librarians.* [Dissertation] Vancouver, B.C.: University of British Columbia.

Buechner, Frederick. (1973). *Wishful thinking: A theological ABC.* New York:Harper & Row

Cappelli, Peter. (1999). *The new deal at work: Managing the market driven workforce.* Boston, Mass.:Harvard Business School Press.

Casson, Lionel. (2001). *Libraries in the ancient world.* New Haven, Conn.: Yale University Press.

Chatman, Elfreda A. (1992, Winter). "The role of mentoring in sharing public library leaders." *Library Trends,* 40(3), 492-512.

Colum, Padraic. (1918). *The adventures of Odysseus and the tale of Troy.* New York: The Macmillan Company.

Cooper, Joanne E. (1991). "Telling our own stories." In C. Witherell and N. Noddings, Eds. *Stories lives tell: Narrative and dialogue in education* (96-112). New York: Teachers College Press.

Cousineau, Phil. (1994). *Soul: An archaeology.* San Francisco: HarperCollins.

Daloz, Laurent A. (1999). *Mentor: Guiding the journey of adult learners.* San Francisco: Jossey-Bass.

Delors, Jacques. (1988). *The treasure within: Report to UNESCO of the International Commission on Education for the Twenty-first Century.* Paris: UNESCO.

De Pree, Max. (1997). *Leading without power: Finding hope in serving community.* Holland, Mich.: Shepherd Foundation.

Derr, C. Brooklyn, Sylvie Roussillion, and Frank Bournois, Eds. (2002). *Cross-cultural approaches to leadership development.* Westport, Conn.: Quorum Books.

Dickinson, Emily. (n.d.) "The Book." In *A book of good poems* (1959), C. T. Fyfe. Toronto, Ontario: Copp Clark.

Dirkx, John M. (1996, Winter). "Human resource development as adult education: Fostering the educative workplace." *New Directions for Adult and Continuing Education,* 72, 41-47.

Dirkx, John M., and Terry Deems. (1996). "Towards an ecology of soul in work: Implications for human resource development." In E. F. Holton III, Ed. *Academy of Human Resource Development 1996 Conference Proceedings* (276-283). Austin, Tex.: Academy of Human Resource Development.

Dirkx, John M. (1997, Summer). "Nurturing soul in adult learning." *New Directions for Adult and Continuing Education,* 74, 79-88.

Duerk, Judith. (1993). *I sit listening to the wind: Woman's encounter within herself.* San Diego, Calif.: LuraMedia.

Eliot, Thomas S. (1925). "The Hollow Men." In *A book of good poems* (1959). C. T. Fyfe. Toronto, Ontario: Copp Clark.

Elkins, David N. (1995, Spring). "Psychotherapy and spirituality: Toward a theory of the soul." *Journal of Humanistic Psychology,* 35(2), 78-98.

Fenwick, Tara. (1998). "Questioning the concept of the learning organization." In S. M. Scott, B. Spencer, and A. M. Thomas, Eds. *Learning for life* (140-152). Toronto, Ontario: Thompson Educational Publishing, Inc.

Fisher, Roger, and Alan Sharp. (1998). *Getting it done: How to lead when you're not in charge.* New York: HarperCollins.

Fleming, Jean Anderson. (1998, Summer). "Understanding residential learning: The power of detachment and continuity." *Adult Education Quarterly*, 48(4), 260-271.

Franklin, Jennifer. (1996, July, August). "An uncommon experience—Northern Exposure to Leadership." *Feliciter*, 14-15.

Fox, Matthew. (1994). *The reinvention of work: A new vision of livelihood for our time.* San Francisco, Calif.:HarperSanFrancisco.

Gilligan, Carol. (1982). *In a different voice.* Cambridge, Mass.: Harvard University Press.

Gemmill, Gary and Judith Oakley. (1992, Feb.). "Leadership: An alienating social myth?" *Human Relations*, 45(2), 113-17.

Grint, Keith, Ed. (1997). *Leadership: Classical, contemporary, and critical approaches.* New York: Oxford University Press, Inc.

Haigh, Susan. (1995). "Northern Exposure to Leadership Institute." *National Library News* (of Canada), (27)1, 5-7.

Hartt, Frederick. (1979). *Michelangelo.* New York: Harry N. Abrams, Inc.

Heshusius, Lous, and Keith Ballard, Eds. (1996). *From positivism to interpretivism and beyond: Tales of transformation in educational and social research.* New York: Teachers College Press, Columbia University.

Hillman, James. (1989). *A blue fire.* New York: Harper & Row Publishers.

Huber, Nancy S. (1998). *Leading from within.* Malabar, Fla.: Keieger Publishing Company.

Kahne, Joseph. (1994, Fall). "Democratic communities, equity, and excellence: A Deweyan reframing of educational policy analysis." *Educational Evaluation and Policy Analysis*, 16(3), 233-248.

Karp, Rashell S., and Cindy Murdock. (1998). "Leadership in Librarianship." In Terrence F. Mech and Gerard B. McCabe, Eds. *Leasdership and Academic Libraries.* Westport, Conn.: Greenwood Press.

Kelly, Robert. (1992). *The power of followership: How to create leaders people want to follow and followers who lead themselves.* New York: Doubleday/Currency.

Kent, Corita. (1997). In R. Fulgrum, *Words I wish I wrote.* New York: HarperCollins.

King Ramses I, circa 1500 B.C., (the oldest known library Motto), "House of Healing for the Soul" as noted in Nicholas A. Basbanes' book *Patience & Fortitude: A Roving Chronicle of Book People, Book Places, and Book Culture*, as cited in *Booklist*, vol. 98, Sept. 15, 2001. (Special thanks to Veronica Healy, Andre Cote, and Mary

Bond of Virtual Reference Canada, Library and Archives Canada for tracing this citation.)

Kozol, Jonathan. (1980). *The night is dark and I am far from home.* New York: Continuum.

Marshall, Catherine, and Gretchen Rossman. (1999). *Designing qualitative research*, 3rd. ed. Thousand Oaks, Calif.: Sage Publications.

Matthews, Caitlin. (1995). *Singing the soul back home: Shamanism in daily life.* Shaftesbury, Dorset: Element Books, Ltd.

Michaelson, Gerald A. (2001). *Sun Tzu: The art of war for managers.* Avon, Mass.: Adams Media Corporation.

Moxley, Russ. (2000). *Leadership and spirit: Breathing new vitality and energy into individuals and organizations.* San Francisco: Jossey-Bass.

Moore, Thomas. (1992). *Care of the soul: A guide for cultivating depth and sacredness in everyday life.* New York: HarperCollins.

Moore, Thomas. (1996a). *The education of the heart.* New York: HarperCollins.

Moore, Thomas. (1996b). *The re-enchantment of everyday life.* New York: HarperCollins.

Muggeridge, Malcolm. (1971). *Something beautiful for God: Mother Teresa of Calcutta.* London: Collins.

Noddings, Nel. (1992). *The challenge to care in schools: An alternative approach to education.* New York: Teachers College Press.

Noddings, Nel. (1995). *Philosophy of education.* Boulder, Colo.: HarperCollins.

*Oxford English Dictionary.* (1933). Oxford: Clarendon Press.

Petit, Michel, and Christian Scholz. (2001). "Highfliers in Germany." In C. Brooklyn Derr, Sylvie Roussillion, and Frank Bournois, Eds. *Cross-cultural approaches to leadership development* (86-108). London: Quorum Books.

Potter, David. (1994). *Prophets and Emperors.* Cambridge, Mass.: Harvard University Press.

Redmond, Layne. (1997). *When the drummers were women: A spiritual history of rhythm.* New York: Three Rivers Press.

Sardello, Robert J. (1985, Spring). "Educating with soul: A phenomenological archetypal reflection on higher education." *Teachers College Record*, 86(3), 423-439.

Sardello, Robert J. (1992). *Facing the world with soul.* New York: HarperCollins.

Scott, Sue. (1997). "The grieving soul in the transformation process." *New Directions for Adult and Continuing Education*, 74, 41-50.

Stone, Irving. (1968). *The agony and the ecstasy.* New York: Doubleday and Co.

Thomas, Dylan. (1952). "Do Not Go Gentle into That Good Night." In *A book of good poems* (1959). C. T. Fyfe. Toronto, Ontario: Copp Clark.

Traquandi, Luciano, and Ratrizia Castellucci. (2002). "Leadership Italian style." In C. Brooklyn Derr, Sylvie Roussillion, and Frank Bournois, Eds. *Cross-cultural approaches to leadership development* (109-122). London: Quorum Books.

Wilde, Oscar. (1911). *De Profundis.* London: Methuen & Co.

Witherell, Carol, and Nel Noddings, Eds. (1991). *Stories lives tell: Narrative and dialogue in education.* New York: Teachers College Press.

Zukav, Gary. (1989). *The seat of the soul.* New York: Simon and Schuster.

# About the Author

Dr. Donna Brockmeyer completed a doctorate in educational leadership and policy at the University of British Columbia in 2000. Her research was based on Northern Exposure to Leadership, which she helped Ernie Ingles to launch after attending Snowbird Leadership Institute in the Wasatch Mountains, Utah, in 1993. She began working in libraries in 1979, prior to completing a high honors degree in sociology in 1989, and an MLIS from the University of Alberta in 1991. She has worked in all types of libraries including academic, public, school and special, from entry to administrative capacities. She teaches, writes and presents on the topics of leadership and soul in the workplace and has been active with many library associations.

Brockmeyer is the Library Director at St. Thomas More College at the University of Saskatchewan in Canada. She lives in Saskatoon, Saskatchewan, with her family, where she blissfully tosses pearls of drunken wisdom into goblets of red wine with her dear and cherished friends.

# On the Cover

The *Sibilla Libica*, or *Libyan Sibyl*, is from the Sistine Ceiling, Vatican, Rome, painted by Michelangelo. Adorned in a superb gown and headdress of golden wisdom and divinity, Sibyl is a strong, virile and graceful prophet who humbly proffers a book describing her vision of the coming of the Messiah. Another of ten mythical renderings of Sibyls, the Cumaean Sibyl, wrote her prophesies in nine books that she offered to sell to Tarquin, the last of seven kings of Rome. He refused the price, and so Sibyl burned first three, and then three more, until he purchased the remaining three for the original price of the nine. Sibyl, while a prophet, was a woman of courage and conviction who believed in the power of her vision and the power of the book in shaping the future of our world. When it is said that leaders, any of us, stand on the shoulders of giants when we do our work, we certainly stand on hers.